DORDT INFORMATION SERVICES
3 6520 0028153 Z

D1156821

LT. COL. JESSE J. JOHNSON (Ret.)
Hampton Institute, Hampton, Virginia

ABOUT THE AUTHOR

Born in Hattiesburg, Mississippi, in 1914, Lieutenant Colonel Jesse J. Johnson earned his B.A. Degree from Tougaloo College, Mississippi, in 1939, his LLB Degree from American Extension School of Law, Chicago in 1950, and served with CCC Camps in Michigan until the early forties. In 1942, he entered the Army as a private, retiring in 1962, with the rank of Lieutenant Colonel after twenty years of military service. In 1964, Colonel Johnson received his M.A. Degree in Education from Hampton Institute, Virginia.

He is author of EBONY BRASS, An Autobiography of Negro officers' frustration amid aspirations, A PICTORIAL HISTORY OF BLACK SOLDIERS (1619-1969), A PICTORIAL HISTORY OF BLACK SERVICEMEN (AIR FORCE, ARMY, NAVY, MARINES), TUMULT' (ROMAN COURT MARTIAL), a play and of several other plays. He became interested in Negro history in elementary school and has long believed that omissions or distortions of the Negro's contribution to U.S. History influences, through ignorances, inter-group friction. EBONY BRASS and other text, are the writer's small contributions toward national goodwill and to the missing pages in U.S. History.

The author invites criticism, suggestions, and comments from readers. He also desires additional photos, photocopies of personal or official letters, data, citations, old newspaper clippings, records, etc., about the male and female Negro military personnel from the Colonial Period to the present. To date, the author has collected several thousand items. Such correspondence should be addressed to Lt. Col. Jesse J. Johnson, Hampton Institute, Hampton, Virginia 23368.

THE BLACK SOLDIER
(Documented) (1619–1815)

MISSING PAGES

IN

UNITED STATES HISTORY

EDITED BY: **JESSE J. JOHNSON**
Lieutenant Colonel, AUS (Ret.)

EDITED AND DISTRIBUTED BY
JESSE J. JOHNSON, Lieutenant Colonel, AUS (Ret.)
Hampton Institute, Hampton, Virginia

Printed in the United States of America

Library of Congress Catalog Card Number: 79-130445

JESSE J. JOHNSON
Lieutenant Colonel, AUS
Hampton Institute
Hampton, Virginia 23368

Second Printing
and
Revised edition

THE BLACK SOLDIER

(Documented) (1619-1815)

By

JESSE J. JOHNSON
Lieutenant Colonel, AUS (Ret.)

THE BLACK SOLDIER

(Documented) (1619-1815)

DEDICATED

TO

the missing pages in U. S. History whose unknown and unherald contents could contribute toward better relationship between different racial groups within the United States.

CONTENTS

CHAPTER 1

CHAPTER 2

CHAPTER 3

CHAPTER 4

CHAPTER 5

CHAPTER 6

FOREWORD
RACE RELATIONS IN THE ARMED FORCES

Racial tensions in the Armed Forces have recently increased; however, to reverse this trend, the Department of Defense has launched the most extensive race relations training program in United States history. The plan to reduce tension is not restricted to white and black relationships but is extended to relationships between the majority and all minority groups.

Secretary of Defense Melvin R. Laird has established an Inter-Service Task Force on Education in Race Relations. This task force is composed of officers and enlisted men of all the services and of all minority groups. Its assigned task is to develop an educational program on race relations for use throughout the Armed Forces. The need to stress accelerated education on race relations and to improve communication has been suggested by the House Armed Services Committee and by other research groups.

In the meantime, the Army has been directed to incorporate race relations in its training program from basic training to all non-commissioned officer and officer training schools, including officers' staff colleges. This is being done. Among comprehensive steps being taken to ease racial tensions, the Army tells all servicemen and officers of the history and contirbutions of all minority groups and of many racial training items heretofore left to chance. If an enlisted man has not been selected for promotion or for desirable duty assignments, he is told why he was not selected or assigned. In addition to other reasons, lack of promotions and desirable assignments have been the source of many complaints among minority groups. Black oriented items are provided in post and base exchanges. Literature, training films, recordings, books, periodicals, etc. relating to blacks and other minority groups are available for official orientation and training. Training manuals and training films are being revised to show minority group individuals demostrating points in training. Open forums and seminars in which all races discuss the race problems, face to face, are scheduled a minumum of once each year throughout the Army on all post levels. Certain key personnel at each post is required to attend these seminars and forums. Positive, firm, but fair command action is required of all commanders. The Air Force, Navy, and Marines are also formulating their race relations training programs.

Prior to 1948, the official policy of the Military Departments was "hands off" any discussions of racial tensions, on or off the military posts or bases. Now the policy is the extreme opposite. Many minority group "old timers" recall much suffering and humiliation under the "hands off" policy. The discussion of racial incidents or potenial friction was then considered as "stirring up racial trouble" by far too many high ranking officers and officials.

Since the issuance of President Trunman's Executive Orders of July, 1948, every President, Congress, and the courts have taken increasing stronger action to implement equal opportunity for all Armed Forces personnel. It is significant to note that, as this is being written, thirteen young men are graduating from Prairie View A & M College, Texas and are being commissioned, in May, 1970, through the first naval R.O.T.C. unit established at a Negro College. While the number of black naval and marine officers has tripled in recent years, they are merely integrating into a "great white fleet." Army and Air Force black officers are less than two percent while enlisted men are ten to twelve percent of the Armed Forces.

Neither segregation nor discrimination has any official backing. For example, segregated off-post housing and facilities can now be placed "off limits." The Civil Rights Act of 1964 was passed by Congress and the Supreme Court desegregation decision of 1954 has been issued. Equality of opportunity in the Armed Forces is now a right by executive, legislative, and judicial policy. Implementation of the new policy into the hearts, attitudes, and daily behavior of officers and servicemen is the job left to be done. It is hoped that this will be done through official educational training in race relations.

The Armed Forces have a race problem because our society has a similar problem. Although the Armed Forces are not an agency for social reform, it is far ahead of other phases of our society in equality of opportunity. Neither the young whites nor the young blacks nor other minority groups servicemen fully realize nor appreciate the progress that has been made since segregation was officially ended in 1948 in the Armed Forces. It is as difficult for young white and Negro servicemen to realize what segregation was really like prior to 1948 as it is for some persons to visualize how dehumanizing slavery really was in 1848. Educating our young people to know our common history requires positive action and can not be left to chance.

The Department of Defense's human goal is to make the military service a model of equal opportunity and it requires all commanders to set the climate for communication, attitudes, and behavior between races in their units.

It is the hope of the editor that the information on these pages will help enchance cultural awareness, improve race relations and strengthen unity between all racial groups.

JESSE J. JOHNSON
LIEUTENANT COL. AUS (RET)
HAMPTON INSTITUTE
HAMPTON, VIRGINIA

INTRODUCTION

The actual history of the Black Soldier did not begin in the United States, as many believe. Herodutus (484-425BC), the father of recorded history, traveled extensively in Asia Minor, Europe, and Africa. He wrote that the Egyptians and the Ethiopians were "black and wooly-haired." These countries had strong, long-lasting armies and cultures. Later, kingdoms in West and East and South Africa developed. Before the arrival of Columbus the existence of darker tribes and of old status in South and Central America, in the Pacific Islands, and in Asia indicates the extent to which the Africans migrated. The black man has contributed to Civil and military aspects of life wherever he has lived. Each continent has had its military heroes. To name a scattered few is sufficient: Hannibal of Carthage (247BC-183BC); Antar, the Lion (Six Century) of Arabia; Malik Amber (1548-1628) of India; Simon Bolivar (1783-1830), liberator, in South America.

After centuries of local freedom and strife in Africa, the black man came to a fate-hounded destiny; the African gods abandoned him to centuries of perials (1540-1865). Strange, blue-eyed, long-haired men, proud in war and trade, came to Africa with ships and guns of slavery. Black men, women, and children were put in chains and exiled to all the continents of the world. Exiled black men now serve in armies of distant land. Thus comes the story of the Afro-American in the Army of the United States.

THE AFRO-AMERICANS IN THE U.S. ARMY

The extent to which Negro slaves and freedmen were utilized as soldiers in the United States from 1619 to 1815 will never be fully known. The number of. records of performance of slaves is naturally limited. A selected number of the available documents are included in this book. The term documents is used, by the editor, broadly, to include records, extracts of state and federal laws, letters, diary extracts, official papers, etc.

During the colonial period, frequent attacks were made upon the British colonists by the Indians, and by competative Europeans. For protection the colonists enacted laws and made plans to recruit and to train men to bear arms for military defense. Most of the Negro population was enslaved. In times of eminent danger, assualts, and invasions the colonists did not hesitate to require their bondmen or freedmen to serve in the Army. Historically, the general practice of untilizing the Negro as a soldier may be characterized as the three "R's"; during peace, reject; during war, recruit; after war, reject. This practice is reflected in correspondence, records of provinces, state, and federal legislative act, military orders, state paper, and official records. Selected excerpts from such documents follow:

> "Act of the General Assembly of Virginia. At a General Assembly 16th Jan. 1639. All persons except Negroes to be provided with arms and ammunition or be fined at pleasure of the Governor and Council. (Hennings Statutes of Virginia, Volume 1, pp. 224, 226)."

As the threat of the Tuscarora War, 1711-1713, with the Indians in South Carolina, in North Carolina, and in Virginia increased, the Assembly of the Province of South Carolina passed, during the period 1703 to 1711, a series of lengthy acts regulating military service of the slaves. A brief excerpt from one of South Carolina's laws follows:

> "XXV. And be it further enacted by authority aforesaid, that it shall and may be lawful for any master or owner of any slave, in actual invasion, to arm and equip any slave or slaves, with such arms and ammunition as any other person...." (Adopted December 23, 1703, Statute at large, S.C. published in 1840, Volume 7, p. 33)

From time to time, the Negro slaves were used by the Colonists as soldier and sailors until the first years of the Revolutionary War.

During the first months of the Revolutionary War, the Negro was not enlisted:

> "Headquarters, Cambridge, November 12, 1775. Parole America-Countersign-Freedom.
>
> Neither Negroes, boys unable to bear arms, nor old men unfit to endure the fatigues of war of the Campaign are to be enlisted.
>
> (Washington's orders, Volume 1 p. 111, State Department)."

During the course of the Revolutionary War, the Negro slaves were promised freedom by the British if they'd join the King's Army. Some slaves, seeking freedom, crossed over to the British side. To counteract this offer, the British colonist proclaimed severe penalities, set up road blocks, and moved many slaves to the interior. In an effort to counteract the British offer, the colonist finally adopted a variety of modified policies to recruit Negroes. The following extract shows the extent to which Negroes were finally used.

> "Extract from the Journal of a Hessian Officer, Schloezer, in the service of King George III October 23, 1777, relating to the use of Negroes in the American Army.
>
> The Negro can take the field instead of his master; and therefore no regiment is to be seen in which there are not Negros in abundance; and among them there are able bodied, strong and brave fellows. (An Historical Research, Livermore, p. 111)."

The Negro was at first rejected, and later recruited during the War of 1812; however, after both the Revoluntionary War and the War of 1812, he was again released and rejected in 1820, as indicated by the following order:

"Adjutant and Inspector
Generals Office
February 18, 1820

General orders

No Negro or Mulatte will be recieved as a recruit of the Army;--------

By order-----------"

If the whole truth about the American Negroes military contribution were ever unearthed, summarized, and revealed on pages of written history to present-day, opened-mined Americans, many racial tensions would be minimized. In todays society ignorance is, to a degree, the trademark of intolerance for the Negro; Appreciation has too often retreated before injustice, irrational responses, and wholesale hostility. The solution to tribal, racial, or other tensions is not easy; however, unified efforts can contribute greatly toward a smoother working relationship. Centuries of tribal and racial friction has occured, however, men have never made a genuine unified effort to end such strife.

This is one of a planned series of documentaries by the editor about thc Negro as a soldier from 1619 to Vietnamese conflict.

The format of this book is planned to help the reader realize maxium benifit from use of the material. Revealing and interesting, the documents are arranged generally in date order and are selected from among thousands on hand.

The selection and arrangement are intended to stimulate interest. The editors introductory comments preceeding each document are purposely brief; Many documents are presented in their entirely; a few are excerpted with efforts to avoid changing their meaning; documents, more or less, repetitious in nature, are omitted. It is hopedthat this format will dispence with a degree of boredom inherent in reading documents. The editors comments are generally in italics and/or in brackets.

These documents are a valuable source of material for the military service, for researchers, for use in universities, colleges, and high schools; and for public officals and the general reader who seeks factural information about the Negro's role in history as revealed in a few of the missing pages of United States History.

JESSE J. JOHNSON
Lt. Col. Ret.
Hampton Institute
Hampton, Virginia

CHAPTER 1

INTRODUCTION OF THE BLACK SOLDIER INTO THE COLONIES

In the Colonies the first Negroes, and many poor Europeans brought to the United States were indentured workers for three to seven years. In 1619 the first Africans were prisoners of war or victims of sea piracy and were protected from slavery by international Law. Land had to be cleared; homes and towns had to be built; crops had to be tilled, and military security had to be established. The chronic need for labor soon taught the colonist that seven years or less was a short period so they extended indentured periods to life for the Negroes.

By 1640, slavery for the Negro was offically and legally established in the colonies. For example, in July 1640, three run-away indentured servants were punished by a Virginia Court. A Dutchman, named Victor, and a Scotchman named James Gregory were sentenced to serve one year beyond their contract period. The Negro named John Punch was sentenced to "serve his said master or his assigns for the time of his natural life here or elsewhere." Other colonies followed Virginia's example of separate and unequal court decisions and legalized slavery. The following is an extract of the court order in the John Punch Case:

"9th July, 1640"

> Whereas Hugh Gwyn hath by order from this Board Brought back from Maryland three servants formerly run away from the said Gwyn, the court doth therefore order that the said three servants shall receive the punishment of whipping and to have thirty stripes apiece one called Victor, a Dutchman, the other a Scotchman called James Gregory, shall first serve out their times with their master according to their Indentures, and one whole year apiece after the time of their service is Expired. By their said Indentures in recomprense of his loss sustained by their absence and after that service of their master is Expired to serve the colony for three whole years apiece, and that the third being a Negro named John Punch shall serve his said master or his assigns for the time of his natural life here or elsewhere."

The following documents indicate the earliest dates relative the arrival of Negroes in the United States.

a. [THE SPANIARD BROUGHT NEGROES TO FLORIDA IN 1565.]

"Though it is commonly said that the first African slaves were brought to the American Colonies by a Dutch ship of war, which landed 20 of them at Jamestown, in 1620, they had, as we have seen, been introduced on the continent by the Spaniards at a much earlier date. Sir John Hawkins, the slave merchant, figures in the Spanish settlement of Florida; he arrived off the coast in 1565. In the same year Henendez covenanted with Phillip II, of Spain, to import into Florida five hundred Negro slaves."

(The Civil War in America, Draper, Vol. 1, p. 100)"

b. [THE DUTCH BROUGHT THE FIRST KNOWN AFRICAN TO THE ENGLISH--SPEAKING COLONIES IN 1619.]

"The majority of writers on American History, as well as most histories on Virginia, from Beverly to Howison, have made a mistake in fixing the date of the introduction of the first slaves. Mr. Beverly, whose history of Virginia was printed in London in 1772, is responsible for the error, in that nearly, all subsequent writers, excepting the laborious and scholarly Bancroft and the erudite Campbell have repeated his mistake. Mr. Beverly, speaking of the burgesses having met the Governor and Council at Jamestown, in May, 1620, adds in a subsequent paragraph, 'In August following a Dutch man-of-war landed twenty Negroes for sale; which were the first of that kind that were carried into the country.' By 'August following,' we would infer that Beverly would have his readers understand that this was in 1620. But Burk, Smith, Campbell and Neill gave 1619 as the date. (History of the Negro Race in America, Williams, Vol. 1 p. 116.)"

c. [AN EXTRACT OF JOHN SMITH'S HISTORY.]

(The above is from manuscripts by John Rolfe incorporated in The History of Virginia, New England and the Summer Isles by John Smith, Book 4.)

"x x xAbout the last of August came in a Dutch man of Warre that sold us twenty Negroesx x x x1619"

THE BLACK INFANTRYMAN
1776-1815

CRISPUS ATTUCKS IN THE BOSTON MASSACRE
March 5, 1770 (Schomberg Collection)

CHAPTER 2

THE BLACK SOLDIER
DURING THE COLONIAL ERA

MILITARY CONFLICTS
1629 - 1705

From 1629 to 1705, war between the British and the Indians, and the British and the French and Indian allies was continuous. The French claimed Canada, the St. Lawrence area, Ohio and West beyond the Mississippi River as far as the Rocky Mountains, based on Verrozzanos discoveries of 1524. The British claimed the area from the Atlantic Ocean to the Allegheny Mountains based on the discoveries, in 1497, of John Cabot in Newfoundland. Borders were in dispute. The British, the French, and the Indians wanted the same land. The Negro had to fight on the side of his captors.

The first slaves were carried into New Amsterdam, now New York, by the Dutch in 1626. In 1641, by law, the Negroes were armed with "a tomahawk and half pike" to help fight murderous Indians. Negroes were also utilized by the Dutch to build breast works to defend the city against the English.

A law is generally passed many years after a long established practice begins. On the other hand, passing a law to stop a practice of the people does not put a sudden end to the habit. For example, in recent history, prohibition and school desegregation has not come to a sudden end. Logically, therefore, using the Negro as a soldier preceeded the law which authorized his use in New York in 1641 and passing a law prohibiting the Negro's use in 1939 in Virginia did not necessarily put a sudden end to the practice.

The need for manpower for defense in the colonies was great, partly because of European wars and because Colonial wars were different from European conflicts. Supplies had to be carried from distant towns and from farms to distant forrest fights. Hospitals were crude; diet was poor, sanitation and medicine lacking, consequently epicemics caused as many casualties as battles. Manpower needs increased as new territory was subdued.

From 1622 to 1644, military conflict with the Indians was continuous. During these military conflicts, the first Negroes arrived in 1619 at Jamestown, Virginia. The Negro was not isolated from the crossfire between Indians and Colonists and competative Europeans; consequently had to help during the conflict.

1.[NEGROES WERE EXEMPTED BY LAW, 1639]

[In view of changing military needs Virginia's Assembly passed a law to prohibit the arming of Negroes. To what extent the law was obeyed is difficult to evaluate. Records of the early colonial and Revolutionary War period do not always reflect race, nor were records always made.]

Act of the General Assembly of Virginia.

At a General Assembly, 6th January, 1639.x x x x x x x x x x x x x x x x x x x x x x x x x x x x x x x x x x x x

All persons except Negroes to be provided with arms and ammunition or be fined at pleasure of the Governor and Council. (Hennings Statutes of Virginia, Vol. 1, pp. 224-226.)

2.[NEGROES IN MASSACHUSETTS HAD TO TRAIN IN THE MILITIA]

(In 1638, the first Negroes were brought to Massachuetts from Bermuda. In 1643, a list was prepared, in Plymouth, of all men capable of bearing arms; it contained the names of Abraham Pearse, a blackmore. In 1652 all Negroes, Indians, and males, with certain exceptions, between sixteen and sixty were required to attend training.

The Massachusetts law of 1660, was still in effect during the King Williams War from 1689-1697. This war, between Britain and France, was fought for control of the Hudson Bay, the St. Lawrence, and Quebec areas and was the extension of a war in Europe. Men could not be easily spared to the colonies; local militia, Negroes and friendly Indians were used to supplement colonial and limited European manpower. Military service of Negroes was required intermittenly into another century.)

"In Massachuetts, in 1652, "Negroes and Indians, and Scotchman" (the indented captives of Cromwell, who had encounted his army at the Battle of Durker), were alike, by law, obliged to train in the Militia. In 1656, the law was altered so as to exempt 'Negroes and Indians;' but again in 1660, a new law required 'every person above the age of sixteen years' to train except certain classes of persons specified; and 'except one servant of every magistrate and teaching elder, and the sons and servants of the Major-General for the time being.'

Those who are curious in tracing the early legislation on the subject will notice the contiuance of this vacillation into the next century.

(An Historical Research, etc. Livermore, p. 124)

3. [MARYLAND'S COLONIST PROVIDED ARMS FOR ALL SERVANTS.]

[In 1634, Ceilus Calvert and a few of his converts settled in Maryland to establish a religious haven. Slavery was introduced the same year. Immediately the Maryland settlers ran into military friction with the Indians and their white colonial Virginia neighbors. Squatters from Virginia claimed part of the land in Maryland. The Negroes had to help defend each colony in which they resided. Virginia's military strife with the Indians from 1622 to 1644 spilled into Maryland because the surviving Indians migrated toward the Great Lake area.]

Act of the General Assembly of Maryland, at a session held at Patuxent, October 20th, 1654.

Concerning the Militia.

It is enacted that there be a Captain and Officers in every county whose office it shall be to take view of Arms in every family and that all persons from sixteen years of age to sixty shall be provided with Serviceable Arms, and Sufficient Ammunition of Powder and Shot ready upon all occasions, and that every master of families provide Arms and Ammunition as aforesaid for Every such Servant, and that the said Capt. so Chosen or appointed have power by Commission Granted him for the Exercising of such persons as Aforesaid and Imploying them for the service of the Commonwealth.

(Proceedings and Acts of the General Assembly of Maryland. Browne, 1637, 1664. p.347.)

4.[ALL PERSONS BETWEEN 16 AND 60 WERE LISTED FOR SERVICE; 1658]

Maryland was established in 1634 on a feudal principle wherein the landowners had many powers similar to the King in England. Slavery began the same year. In 1658, official action to secure these holdings militarly was taken by the colonial council. They required a list of all persons able to bear arms between sixteen and sixty. Military friction over boundaries between Maryland and Virginia continued.)

Proceedings of the Council of Maryland.
At a Council held at Wicocomaco June 3, 1658.
Ordered. x x x x
(Organization of the Militia.)

When not taken into consideration the settlement of the Militia

Province & certain Instruction were drawne up to be sent to the several divisions & Commissions ordered to be drawne for them also viz:x x x

Imprimis that they cause a perfect list to be taken of all persons able to bear Arms within their respective divisions that is of all men between 16 and 60 years of Age which list they are to return to the Governor or Secretary with all convenient speed.

(Proceedings of the Council of Maryland. Browne 1636-1667. pp. 344-345.)

5. [NEGROES IN NEW JERSEY WERE NOT EXEMPTED, 1668.]

[New Jersey had a few settlers as early as 1614. The Negro was *introduced as a slave into New Jersy in 1628. Religious conflict and scattered military contests exsisted between the Colonists and the Indians. The Negro slave was caught in the crossfire. The Act of the New Jersy General Assembly of 1668 did not exempt Negroes form military training. In actual practice, they probably served much earlier inasmuch as work on farms and in forests exposed the Negroes to Indians.]*

Act of the General Assembly of the Province of New Jersy.

In order to the better providing for the Peace and safety of the Inhabitants of the province, and the more ready accustoming our soldiers to an expert handling of their arms, it is Enacted, that the Soldiers in every Town within this Province from Sixteen Years old to Sixty, shall Train or be Mustered x x x x x

But -x- -x- -x- -x- Passed at the General Assembly begun November 3, 1668.

(Laws of New Jersey, Aaron Leaming and Jacob Spicer, p. 85.)

*Here follow exemptions, in which Negroes and persons of color are not included.

6.[A LIST OF RHODE ISLANDS EXCEPTIONS DID NOT INCLUDE NEGROES.]

(Negroes were brought to the Rhode Island Colony in 1647. In 1636, Roger Williams, who advocated separation of church and state, was

driven from Massachusetts to the wilderness in Rhode Island. Advocating relgious tolerance, he also opposed mistreating the slaves and the Indians. By 1665, a law to train freedmen and bondmen militarily was passed by the colony's General Assembly.]

Act of the General Assembly of Rhode Island Providence Plantation.

The assembly taking into consideration the great defect in training, occasioned by the remissness of some under the pretence of the burden in training so often as eight days in the years, and other complaining of the great inequality, in that the poorest being unable to spare wherewith to maintain arms and ammunition, as powder etc. still are forced by law to bear arms as well as the most able; to redress which grievances it is enacted and declared. x x x

And for the encouragement of the meaner sort, there shall be allowed yearly nine shillings in current pay to or for each soldier listed in the train band, to be duly payed and discounted yearly by the Clerk Treasurer of the train band, at the Captains discretion for the repairing of arms, &c; and the said nine shillings yearly to be payed and cleared by or before the last Monday in March, and delivered or ordered to such parents and masters as finds arms and ammunition (as they must do) for their sones and servants that are listable, which are to be listed, and to train; as also to such householders or other men that find themselves arms and train in their own persons; which all men from sixteen years old are hereby required to do, both masters, parents, sones, servants and others, except such as are in public office or are by other laws exempted;x x x x x x x x x x x x x x x x x x x x x x x x x x x x x x x x x x
The exceptions not including Negroes x x x x

(Passed at session sitting at Newport, May 3, 1665)
(Records of Rhode Island. Vol. 2. p.114)

7.[NEGROES IN CONNECTICUT WERE REQUIRED TO SERVE.]

[In 1636, *Reverand Thomas Hooker and a group of his followers were forced from Massachusetts to the Connecticut Valley due to religious intolerance. During the same year, slavery was introduced. From 1636 to 1689, Military Conflict existed between the French in Canada and the English in Massachusettes and Connecticut. The Negro was required to serve by law in 1672, and,* possibly, *by practice much* earlier.]

The General Laws and Liberties of Connecticut Colonies: Revised and Published by Order of the General Court held at Hartford, in October 1672. x x x x

*Military Officers.

That the Militia may be so managed as may best advantage the Public Weal and Safety of this Colony.

It is Ordered by this Court and the Authority thereof; That all male persons of the age from sixteen years of age, to the age of sixty (except Magislatrates, Church officers, allowed Physicians and Cgyourgeons, School Masterss, Millers, constant Herdsmen, and Mariners, who make it their constant business to go to sea) shall bear Arms unless they upon just occasions have exemption granted them by the Court. x x x x

Laws of Connecticut - Reprint of edition of 1673, by George Bimley, Hartford, 1665, p.49.

8.[THE LAW PROVIDING FOR OBJECTORS WAS VOIDED.]

[Since religion was a primary concern of both Church and State during the colonial era, the matter of conscientious objectors was of importance. The Negro was brought to Rhode Island in 1647. The casual reader is generally inclined to consider conscientious objectors as a "new breed." The religion of a slave in some colonies was not recognized because all Christains were sometimes legally freed. Some men pretended to be conscientious objectors to escape military duty, so the law was voided.]

Act of the General Assembly of the Colony of Rhode Island, and Providence Plantations, at its session begun May 2, 1676.

June the 30th,x x xVoted, that whenever there is a clause made at an assembly held May the 7th, 1673, wherein is specified that persons declaring that it is against their conscience or judgement to bear arms in maritial or military manner, that such shall be liable to the military authority, nor any ways liable to pay the fine by law afore ordained and set; and finding that several, under pretence decline their duty, whereby great disturbance is in the several Train Bands; therefore for the encouragement of the Militia in this Colony, the said clause in the said law is made void, null and repealed. And all persons in this Colony are to be observant actively or passively, as the former laws provided in Military affairs, and this to stand in force, and law or laws, clause or clauses therein to the contrary notwithstanding.

(Records of R.I. vol. 2, p. 549.)

9.[EACH PERSON MUST PROVIDE HIS OWN GUN.]

[Having been in New Jersey since 1628, the Negro had to participate in defence against Indians and dispute between colonists. The English seized New Jersey and New York in 1664 from the Dutch. In 1668 and again in 1682 all men "from sixteen years old onto sixty" were required to serve in the colonial militia. Military friction existed between New York and New Jersey over boundaries and authority to rule one or both colonies by New York. Many Quakers settled in New Jersey and they were hostile toward slavery.]

Act of the General Assembly of East New Jersey

At the General Assembly begun and holden at Elizabeth Town in the Province of East New Jersey the first day of March, Anno Domini, 1682.

AN ACT OF THE MILITIA

Foreasmuch as it is requistie, and of necessity amonst all men to be in a posture of Defence against Enemies or Dangers that may accure, especially by the insolence and outrages of the Heathen as of late hath been in our neighbouring Colonies. Be it therefore Enacted by this present Assembly, and Authority of the same, that every male within this Province from sixteen years old unto sixty, be provided at his own cost and charge, with a good sufficient Fire Lock Gun. Be it further enacted by the Authority aforesaid, that there shall be four days in a Year for Training, or Mustering.

At which time all the Males from sixteen years old unto sixty having sufficient warning from the Captain of Each Company, shall make their appearance in complete Arms, at the time and place appointed for discipling the said Company (excepting Magistrates, Ministers, Deputies, Constables) in default whereof for the late coming at the time appointed, every such person shall pay by the way of fine six-pence, for half a day absence, fifteen pence, and for total absence from said training, three shillings; the same to be levied by way of destraint upon refusal of payment as above specified x x x

(Laws of New Jersey, Aaron Leaming and Jacob Spicer, pp. 256-277)

10.[ALL PERSONS MUST ATTEND MILITARY TRAINING,1685.]

[All men, including Negroes, between sixteen and sixty years of age were required by law to attend all military trainings in new Plymouth, as early as 1643. In 1630 Negroes were introduced into Massachusetts. By practice, and by law all men generally had to defend against French and Indian attacks and help during local colonial military disputes. Slavery was abolished in Massachusetts in 1780.]

Enactment of the "Inhabitants of the Jurisdiction of New Plimouth."

Military Affairs.

For the better regulating the Military Forces of this Colony, and Training our Souldery for such service as they may be called into; 2. It is ordered that all Men between sixteen and sixty years of age constantly attend all Military Training when duly warned. x x x x x x

(General Laws of the Inhabitants of the Jurisdiction of New Plimouth. Printed by "Order and Authority of the General Court of New Plimouth held at Plimouth, June 2nd, 1685. p. 51.)

11.[NEGROES AND INDIANS WERE EXEMPTED;1693]

[The King William War (1689-1697) was fought for control of the North Eastern area of what is now the United States and Canada. Negroes and Indians were provided arms and ammunition only, without being subjected to formal military training.]

Act of the General Court of the Province of Massachusetts Bay.

An Act for regulating of the Militia.

Whereas, for the honor and service of their majesties, and for the security of this their province against any violence or invasion whatever, it is necessary that due care be taken that the inhabitants thereof be armed, trained and in a suitable posture and readiness x x x

Be it therefore enacted by His Excellency the Governor, Council and Representatives in General Court Assembled, and it is ordained and enacted by the authority of the same.

(Sec. 1) That all male persons from sixteen years of age to sixty (other than such as hereinafter excepted), shall bear arms and duly attend all musters and military exercises of the respective troops and companies where they are enlisted or belong, allowing three month's time to every son next after coming to sixteen years of age, x x x x x

(Section 12.) That the persons hereafter named be exempted from all trainings, viz: -x--x- Indians and Negroes. x x x x

(Section 26.) That all persons exempted by this law from training shall, notwithunderstanding, be provided with arms and ammunition complete, upon the same penalty as those that are obliged to train.

Adopted November 22, 1693.

(Acts and Resolves of the Province of Massachusetts Bay, Vol. 1, pp. 128,130,133.)

12.[ALL SERVANTS ARE PROVIDED WITH ARMS,1702.]

[The Queen Anne's War (1702-1713) was a renewal of hostilities between France and England for control over disputed area in Canada, Massachusetts, New York, and in the St. Lawrence River areas. All servants were reqiured in New Jersey to be provided with arms in 1702. Believing in respect for all peoples, as Quakers, every element of the population had to do its share of military duty. The Quakers population considered slavery as violence.]

All Planters and Christian Servants are Provided with Arms by Original Constitution, 1702

Instruction for our Rightfully and well beloved Edward Lord Cornbury, our Captain General and Governor in Chief in and over our Province, Nova Caesarea or New Jersey, in America. Given at our Court at St. James, the 16th day of November, 1702, in the first year of our Reign.

With these our Instructions you will receive our Commission under our Great Seal of England constituting you our Captain General and Governor in Chief of our Province of New Jersey.xxxx

You shall take care that all planters and Christian servants be well and fitly provided with arms, x x x x

The General Concessions, and Original Constitution of the Province of New Jersey, etc., Leaming and spicer, pp.619-634)

13.[THE NEGROES ARE USED AS SOLDIERS.]

[South Carolina had a population of two slaves for each colonist; Negro slaves during emergencies for military defense. Numerous

legislative acts were passed to regulate the use of slaves in such defense. The two acts below illustrate the detailed legislation passed by South Carolina. The Queen Anne's War (1702-1713) in the north was being fought when these statutes were passed. From 1711-1713, South Carolina was involved in the Tuscarora War assisting North Carolina against the Indians.]

a. Act of the General Assembly of the Province of South Carolina, 1703.

An additional Act to an Act entitled 'An Act to prevent the Sea's further encroachment upon the Warfe, at Charles Town' and for the repairing and building more Batterys and Flankers on the said wall to be built on the said Warfe; and also for the fortifying the remaining parts of Charles Town by intrenchments, Flankers and Pallisades, and appointing a garrison to the Southward. x x x x x x x

XXIII. Whereas, it is necessary for the safety of this colony in case of actual invasions, to have the assistance of our trusty slaves to assist us against our enemies, and it being reasonable that the said slave should be rewarded for the good service they may do us, Be it therefore enacted by the authority aforesaid, That if any slave shall, in actual invasion, kill or take one or More of our enemies, and the same shall prove by any white person to be done by him, shall, for his reward, at the charge of the publick have and enjoy his freedom for such his taking or killing as aforesaid; and the master or owner of such slave shall be paid and satisfied by the publick, at such rates and prices as three freeholders of the neighborhood who well know the said slave, being nominated and appointed by the Right Honorable the Governor, shall award, on their oaths, and if any of the said slave happen to be killed in actual service of this Province by the enemy, then the master or owner shall be paid and satisfied for him in such manner and forme as is before appointed to owners whose Negroes are set free.

XXIV. And be it further enacted by the authority aforesaid, that if any slave aforesaid is wounded in the service aforesaid, so that he is disabled for service to his master or owner then such slave so disabled shall be set free at the charge of the publick, in such manner and forme as aforesaid is provided, and shall also be maintained at the charge of the said publick.

XXV. And be it further enacted by the authority aforesaid, That it shall and may be lawful for any Master or owner of any slave, in actual invasion, to arme and equip any slave or slaves with such arms and ammunition as any other person by the act of Militia are appointed to appear at Muster or Alarms.

Adopted December 23, 1703.

(Statutes at Large, S.C., pub. in 1740, Vol. 7, p. 33.)

b. Act of the Assembly of the Province of South Carolina:

An Act for the raising and enlisting such slaves as shall be thought serviceable to this Province in time of alarms.

Whereas, among the several slaves belonging to this Colony, there are a great number of them who, by care and discipline, may be rendered serviceable toward the defense and preservation of this province, in Case of actual invasion, in order, therefore, to make the assistance in our said trusty Slaves more certain and regular;

I. Be it enacted by his Excellency John P. Granville, Paliatine, and the rest of the true and absolute lords and proprietors of this Province, by and with the advice and consent of the rest of the members of the General Assembly, now met at Charlestown, for the southwest part of this Province, and by the authority of the same, That within thirty days after ratification of this Act, the several captains or commanders of companies throughout this province do, by virtue of a warrant under their hands and seals, impower and commissionate five freeholders in their respective divisions (being sober, discreet men) to form and complete a list of such Negroes, Mulatoes and Indian slaves, as they, or any three of them, shall judge serviceable for the purpose aforesaid; which said commissioners, after having finished their said list, are to warn and summons the master, mistresses or overseers to whom the said slaves do belong, to appear before them at a certain day, to show cause (if any) why their said slave or slaves so chosen, should not continue in the said list, of which reasons, the said commissioners, or any three of them, are hereby made competent judges, to allow or disapprove, as they in their discretion shall think fit; and futher to direct and require the several masters, mistresses or overseers of the said slaves, on time of alarm or other special summons, that they cause their several slaves so enlisted, and armed either with a serviceable lance, hatchet or gun, with sufficient ammunition and hatchets, according to the conveniency of the said owners, to appear under the coulors of the respective captains, in their several divisions, throughout the Province, there to remain and be disposed in such manner as the said officers or the commander-inchief shall direct and appoint, for the public service.

III... And be it further enacted by the authority aforesaid, That if any slaves enlisted as aforesaid shall happen to be killed or mamed in actual service, by the enemy, then the master or owner of such slave so killed or mamed, as aforesaid, shall be satisfied and paid for the same, by the public, at such rate and value as three freeholders of the neighborhood, appointed by the Governor, on their oaths, shall award; on which award so returned, the Governor is hereby impowered to order the receiver to pay the same.

. IV...And be it further enacted,That this Act and everything therein contained, shall continue in force two years, and no longer.

(State, at large, S. S.C. ,Pub. in 1840, Vol. 7, pp. 347, 348,349.) Passed November 4, 1704.

14. [NEGROES MUST SERVE]

[The Negro was brought into North Carolina in 1669 and was not freed until the end of the Civil War. From 1711 to 1713 the Tuacarora War was fought in North Carolina; from 1715 to 1718, the Yemasie War was fought in South Carolina. These were wars between colonists and Indians. In 1715 the North Carolina law required all freemen and servants to serve in the militia. These conflicts were extensive and caused much loss of life. The Indians had French allies in the Northern areas and Spanish allies in the Southern areas were also involved.

The Yemasies, were joined by the Muskogees, the Appalachins, Catawobos, Congarees and Cherokees. All Indians between Virginia and Florida banded together. The Indians were driven southward. North Carolina required all men to serve in the militia in 1715.]

Act of the General Assembly of the Province of North Carolina

An Act for establishing a Militia in this Province. 1. Whereas a Militia may be necessary for the Defense and Safety of this Province: 2. Be it Enacted by the Governor, Council Assembly and by the Authority of the same, That all freemen and servants within this Province, between the age of Sixteen and Sixty, shall compose the Militia thereof. (North Carolina Revision of Laws 1715-1775--pp. 434-5 Passed at session begun and held Nov. 3, 1766

THE BLACK SOLDIER
AND
MILITARY CONFLICT
1705-1775

[From about 1705 to about 1775, the utilization of the freemen and bondmen fluctuated, depending, to a degree, on the military necessity. For example, while the Queen Anne's War (1702-1713) raged in the North Eastern colonies, the Virginia assembly in 1705, exempted Negro slaves. Massachusetts, in 1707, required free Negroes to serve while Maryland legislature exempted all Negroes and slaves in 1719.

When the War shifted during the Tuscarora War (1711-1713) from the North Eastern Colonies to North Carolina, Connecticut excluded Indians and Negroes. In 1723, Virginia Negroes were used as drummers and trumpeters and as laborers to support the military defense.

While the King George's War was being fought for control of Canada and the Mississippi Valley, (1745-1748), New Jersey passed an act in 1746 to recruit five hundred free men and Indians to fight in Canada. After this War, in 1750, Connecticut excluded Negroes and Indians.

The French and Indian War (1749-1760) was fought in Canada, along the Mississippi River, and on the Gulf of Mexico. In 1756 Virginia authorized Negroes to be recruited, without arms, as drummers, trumpeteers or pioneers. A pioneer is one who goes before to remove an obstacle.

Thus to a large extent the colonist, legislated the use of Negroes depending on the military situation. In practice, the Negro was probably always involved, being on exposed plantations, if not in military duties certainly in non-military support.]

15. [THE NEGRO SLAVE WAS EXEMPTED.]

Act of the General Assembly of Virginia.

An Act for settling the Militia.

For the settling, arming and training a Militia for Her Majesties service, to be ready on all occasions for the defense and preservation of this Her Colony and dominions.

Be it enacted by the Governor, Council and Burgesses, of this present General Assembly, and it is hereby enacted by the authority of the same. That from and after the publication of this Act, the Colonel or chief Officer of the Militia of every county have full power and authority to list all male persons whatsoever, from sixteen to sixty years of age within his respective county, to serve in horse or foot,x x x xprovided nevertheless, That nothing herein contained shall be construed to give power or authority to any Colonel or Chief Officer whatsoever, to list any person that shall be, or shall have been of Her Majesty's Council in this Colony. x x x x or any slave, but that all and every such person or persons be exempted from serving either in horse or foot. x x x x x x

Passed at session of the General Assembly begun October 23, 1705. (Hennings Statutes of Virginia, Vol. 3, pp. 335-6.)

16. [NEGROES WERE REQUIRED TO SERVE IN 1707 BY LAW]

Act of the General Court of the Province of Massachusetts Bay:

An Act for the regulating of free Negroes, Etc.

Whereas in the several towns and precincts with in this province there are several free Negroes and mulattos, able of body, and fit for labour, who are not charged with trainings, watches, and other services required of her Majesty's subjects, whereof they have share in the benefit. x x x x x x x x

Sec. 3. And be it further enacted that all free male Negroes or Mulattos, of the age of sixteen years and upwards, able of body, in case of alarm, shall make their appearance at the parade of the military company of the precinct wherein they dwell, and attend such service as the first commission officer of such company shall direct, during the time the company continues in arms, on pain of forfeiting the sum of twenty shillings to the use of the company, or performing eight days labour as aforesaid, without reasonable excuse made and accepted for not attending. (Passed June 12, 1707. Acts and Resolves of the Province of Mass. Bay, Vol. 1, pp. 606, 607).

17. [ALL NEGROES WERE EXEMPTED].

Act of the General Assembly of the Province of Maryland.

An Act for the ordering and regulating the Militia of this Province, for the better Defense and Security thereof. x x x

And be it enacted by the Authority aforesaid that all Negroes and Slaves whatsoever shall be exempted the Duty of Training or other Military Service. x x x

Passed June 3, 1715. Continued for three years, by Act of 1719, an further continued withour limitation by Act of 1722.

Bacons Laws of Maryland at Large, 1715. Chap. XL111)

18.[THE NEGRO WAS INCLUDED IN MUSTERS FOR TRAINING]

Act of General Court of the Colony of Connecticut.
An Act for Regulating the Militia.

x x x x x x x

Be it therefore Enacted by the Governor, Council and and Representatives, in General Court Assembled, and it is Ordained and Enacted by the Authority of the Same: 1. That all male persons from sixteen years of age, to sixty (except xxxxIndians and Negroes) shall bear Arms and duly attend all Musters and Military Exercises of the respective Troops and Companies where they are Listed or Belong. x x x Act and Laws of His Majesties Colony of Connecticut in New England. New London, 1715, page 78. (Date of Enactment not given, but prior to October 14, 1708, as shown by Amendment recorded in same volume.)

19.[ALL PERSONS SHALL BEAR ARMS]

Act of the General Assembly of the Colony of Rhode Island and Providence plantation. Laws... Made and Passed by the General Assembly of His Majestics Colony of Rhode Island and Providence Plantations in New England begun and held at Newport the Seventh day of May, 1718. And Continued by Adjourment to the Ninth Day of September following.

x x x x x x x

Be it therefore enacted by the General Assembly of this Colony and by the Authority of the same, and it is hereby Enacted. That all Acts heretofore made Relating to the Militia or appointing Officers of the same, Be hereby and Absolutely Repealed and Declared Null and Void, and that for the future the following Order, Regulation, and Rules Relating to the same, be Kept and Observed by all Persons in this Colony.

First it is Enacted and appointed, that all Male Persons Residing for the space of Three Months within this Colony, from the Age of Sixteen to the Age of Sixty Years, shall bear Arms in their Respective Train Bands, or Companies whereto by law they shall belong Excepting only.-------(Negroes were not exempted.)

And be it further Enacted by the Authority aforesaid. That upon any Alarm in time of War, or other eminent danger of any Assault or Invasion, all Male Persons, both listed Soldiers and others in this colony of and between theAge of Sixteen and Sixty, shall upon notice of the same, forthwith Repair to the Colors and Ensigns of such Company, within whose Province they Inhabit or dwell.

Acts of His Majestics Colony of Laws of Rhode Island and Providence Plantations in America, pp. 85-86. (Passed in May 7, 1718)

20.[THE NEGROES ARE REQUIRED TO DO LABOR]

An act for the settling and better regulation of the Militia.

1. Whereas a due regulation of the Militia is absolutely necessary for the defense of this country, and the act now in force doth not sufficiently provide for the same. II. Be it therefore enacted by the Lieutenant Governor, Council, and Burgesses, of this present General Assembly and it is hereby enacted by the authority of the Laws, That from and after the publication of this act, the colonel or chief officer of the militia of every county, have full power and authority to list all free male persons whatsoever, from twenty-one to sixty years of age, within his respective county.

x x x x x x x

IV. Provide nevertheless that nothing herein contained, shall impower or enable any colonel or commander in chief, to list, or cause to be listed or any free Negro, Mulatto, or Indian.

V. Provided always, that such free Negroes, Mulattos, or Indians, as are capable may be listed and employed as drummers or trumpreters; And that upon any invasions, in or rebellion all free Negroes, Mulattos, or Indians, shall be obliged to attend and watch with the militia and to do the duty of pioneer, or such other senile labor as they shall be directed to perform.

Passed at session begun May 9, 1723.

(Hennings Statutes of Virginia, Vol. 4, pp. 118-119.)

21.[FREEMEN WERE RECRUITED, 1746.]

An Act to encourage the Inlisting of Five Hundred Freemen, or native well affected Indians in this Colony of New Jersey, for his Majesty's service in the present expedition against Canada, for making provision their subsistence for four months, for transporting them to Albany, in the Province of New York; and for Defraying the Expense thereof, out of the Interest Money arising from the Loans of the Bills of Credit of this Colony. x x x x x

2. Now for the encouragement of Five Hundred Freemen or native well affected Indians, to enlist within this Colony, as Soldiers, for the said service, and for answering his Majesty's just expectations, as to the supplying them Provisions, be it Enacted by the Honorable John Hamilton, Esq., President of his Majesty's Council,Commander in Chief of this colony of New Jersey, the council and General Assembly, and it is hereby exacted by the authority of the same, that there shall be paid to every Freeman, or native well affected Indian, who shall enlist either as Sergeant, Corporal, Drummer, Private Soldier, the sum of six pounds proclamation Money over and above His Majesty's pay. x x x x x x x

5. And be it enacted by the Authority Aforesaid, that it shall not be lawful to enlist any young Men under the age of Twenty-one years, or any slaves who are so for Term of Life, bought Servants, or apprentices, without the express leave in writing of thier Parents or Guardians, Masters or Mistresses, first had and obtained. x x x x

(Nevill's Acts of New Jersey, Vol. 1, pp. 314,316)

(Passed June 27,1746) x x x x

22.[THE NEGROES WERE EXEMPTED.]

Act of the General Court of the Colony of Connecticut.

An Act for Forming and Regulating the Militia; and for the Encouragement of Military Skill for the Better defense of this Colony.

Be it Enacted by the Governor, Council and Representatives, in Court Assembled, and by the authority of the same. x x x x

Be it further Enacted by the Authority aforesaid, That All Male Persons from Sixteen years of Age to Fifty, shall bear Arms and duly attend all Musters, and Military Exercises, of the Respective Troops, and Companies where they are Enlisted or do Belong. (Except x x x x x x and Indians and Negroes.) (Acts and Laws of His Majesty's English Colony of Connecticut in New England, In America, New London, pub. 1750, pp. 155-157.)

23.[THE NEGROES SERVE AS DRUMMERS, IN VIRGINIA.]

Act of the General Assembly of Virginia.

An Act for the better regulation and disciplining the Militia.

. x x x x x

II. And be it further enacted by the authority aforesaid, That a lieutenant, or in his absence the chief officer of the militia, in every county, except the county of Hampshire, shall list all male persons over the age of eighteen years, and under the age of sixty years, within this colony (imported servants excepted) under the command of such captain as shall think fit, within one month after the passing of this Act.

x x x x x x x x

VII. And be it further enacted by the authority aforesaid, That all such free Mulattoes, Negroes and Indians as are or shall be enlisted, as aforesaid, shall appear, without arms, and may be employed as drummers, trumpeters, or pioneers, or in such other servile labor as they shall be directed to perform. x x x x

Passed at Session begun 1756, and continued by sundry Acts to July, 1773. (Hennings Statutes of Virginia, Vol. 7, pp. 93-95.)

A list of my Negroes on my Plantations in Albemarle County continued 1 Jany 1770.

39 Punch

40 America Died July 1773 —

41.. Charles

42.. Sawney Died June 1775

43.. Thornton

44.. Jim Died July 1774

45.. Young George

46.. Bob

47.. Isaac

48.. Judy born Jany 19th 1754.

49 Jean born May 2^d 1757.

A SLAVE BOOK PAGE
1770-1775

A SLAVE DWELLING
From State Department of Archives and History, Raleigh, N.C.

CHAPTER 3

THE NEGRO SOLDIER DURING THE REVOLUTIONARY WAR 1776-1781

As a result of the French and Indian War, the English Won, in 1763, France's North American colonies in Canada and in the Mississippi Valley. From 1776 to 1783, the colonists rose up against England, and, with the help of France, became independent. The military conflict is known as the Revolutionary War. The Negro participated as soldiers, sailors, and as civilians, during this war.

The Revolutionary War had its beginning in early policies of the mother country. England regarded the colonies as a place from which to draw raw materials, and, as settlements grew, a place to sell consumer goods manufactured in England.

Charters and laws were designed to benefit England at the expense of the colonists. Among these laws were the Navigation Acts, which required the goods of the colonists to go through England for sale to European countries. The colonies were not permitted to develop their own factories. The Stamp Act, the requirement to house and feed English Soldiers, were also sources of great aggravation to the colonists. Being in bondage, Negroes understood England's oppressive acts, and also wanted freedom.

At first, trade restrictions were not well enforced because England was too busy, until 1763, with various wars. These wars had been costly to England; after 1763 England began to enforce trade restrictions to make the colonies help pay for the war debts as well as commerce. Restrictions became increasingly irritating to the colonists. In the colonies agitation for better laws spread, at first, for fairer laws. The English did not yield to the colonists' complaints. In time, the colonists became increasingly active in their resistance to British rule. Demonstrators became more vocal and active.

Many historians conclude that the fight for American independence really began on March 5, 1770 when the blood of Crispus Attucks, a Negro, and four caucasian colonists was shed upon the streets of Boston. The dead men were regarded as heroes, and a public funeral, well attended, was given them. The war lasted several years. In the battles of Concord Bridge, Bunker Hill, minor encounters, and in many other conflicts, the Negroes participated, at first, in a limited way, and later in a more general manner. The Negroes also hoped to share in the Revolutionary war aims of freedom.

On September 5, 1774, the First Continental Congress met in Philadelphia. These delegates sent a sent a letter to England listing their grievances and published a Declaration of Rights. The English planned to arrestthe signers; however, the plan was leaked to the colonists. Men, like Paul Revere, rode through the night notifying the colonists that the British were coming. Calling themselves Minutemen, a group alerted the colonists, to fight British soldiers. Minutemen and colonists, including Negroes fought from behind trees, bushes, and ditches, like Indians; however, the English fought in straight formations. The colonists won their first victory at Concord Bridge. The news of victory spread among the colonists; this elevated their spirit to fight.

Meanwhile, the Second Continental Congress, held in Philadelphia May 10, 1775, voted to raise an army. George Washington was sworn in as Commander of the untrained volunteers. The Negroes, at first, were rejected by the New Army, except those already in the Colonial Militia.

The ground war raged from the Canadian border to Georgia primarily along the Atlantic coast line. Generally integrated by necessity with other soldiers, an estimated 5000 Negroes, on record, served during the Revolutionary War. According to records, Negroes served from Massachusetts, Vermont, New Hampshire, Rhode Island, Connecticut, New York, New Jersey, Pennsylvania, Maryland, Virginia, North Carolina, and even from the French Island, San Domingo.

The following extract illustrates how widespread Negroes were eventually used as soldiers.

Extract from the Journal of a Hessian officer. October 23, 1777, relating to the use of Negroes in the American Army.

> *"The Negro can take the field instead of his master; and therefore no regiment is to be seen in which there are not Negroes in abundance, and among them there are able-bodied strong and brave fellows."*

The Negro was also used extensively in non-military duties. At the end of the Revolutionary War the population of the Republic was more than 3 million, including about 500,000 Negro slaves. The large number of Negroes demonstrates clearly the Negroes importance during the expanding era. The largest cities were Philadelphia, New York, Boston, Charleston, and Baltimore. Most Americans were farmers, considered rude, rough and living in discomfort. Roads and schools were poor, naval vessels were few, stagecoaches were uncomfortable. Manufacturing and shipping were weak. A peaceful period (1781-1812) made it possible for European immigration and slave importation to increase. In a few years, all aspects of life expanded; the migration of

U.S. citizen was westward, northwest, and southward. Neither the French nor the British could effectively block the expansion of the United States. England did not give up her loss of the American colonies easily so continued to harass the U. S. ships at sea. The harassment was one of the reasons for the War of 1812.

The Negro was rejected at the beginning of the Revolutionary War; reluctantly utilized during the war; and at the end of the War was again rejected, until the critical period of the War of 1812-1815.

The Negro benefitted by the new impetus for freedom and equality so recently won. Organized groups, especially the Quakers, protested against slavery. Such protests eventually affected the status of slavery before,during, and at the end of the Civil War. The Quakers were among the first to advocate the abolition of slavery.

AFRICAN BACKGROUND
A Congolese Family

24.[THE FIRST CASUALTY FOR U.S. INDEPENDENCE WAS A NEGRO]

CRISPUS ATTUCKS,THE FIRST PATROIT-1770

When the United States joined the family of Nations there were in the Country about half a million persons of African descent. Nearly all were slaves; although there were a few, especially in the Eastern States, who had been emancipated. Some of them bore an honorable part in the War of Independence. Crispus Attucks, a colored Patriot, was a leader and the first martyr in the Boston Massacre, on the 5th of March, 1770. One of that race mingled his blood with the fallen patriots of the 19th of April 1775. The sons of Africa fought side by side with their countrymen of the white race at Bunker Hill, where Major Pitcairn, as he stormed the works fell, mortally wonded by the shot of Salem, a black soldier. Indeed it is hardly too much to say that some of the most heroic deeds of the War of Independence were performed by black men. (Wilson's Rise and Fall of the Slave Power) Vol. 1,p.18.

CRISPUS ATTUCK'S MURDERERS WERE TRIED

[The following are excerpts of a verbatim, short-hand recording of the trial of British soldiers who murdered Crispus Attucks, Negro, and four caucasians, Samuel Gray, Samuel Marverick, James Caldwell, and Patrick Carr, on Monday evening, March 5, 1770. Note: Underlines were written in by the editor for emphasis].

TRIAL OF THE BRITISH SOLDIERS

At his Majesty's Superior Court of Judicature, Court of Assize and general Goal Delivery, begun and held at Boston, within, and for the County of Suffolk, on the second Tuesday of March, in the tenth year of the reign of George the Third, by the Grace of GOD, of Great-Britain, France and Ireland, King, Defencer of the Faith, &c.

The Jurors for the said Lord the King, Upon their oath present, that Thomas Preston, Esq. William Wemms, labourer, James Hartegan, labourer, William M. Cauley, labourer, Hugh White, labourer, Matthew Killroy, labourer, William Warren, labourer, John Carrol, labourer, and Hugh Montgomery, labourer, all now resident in Boston, in the county of Suffolk, and Hammond Green, boat builder, Thomas Greenwood, labourer, Edward Menwaring, Esq. and John Munroe, gentlemen, all of

Boston aforesaid, not having the fear of God before their eyes, but being moved and seduced by the instigation of the devil and their own wicked hearts, did on the fifth day of this instant March, at Boston aforesaid, within the county aforesaid, with force and arms, feloniously, willfully, and of their malice aforethought, assault one Crispus Attucks, then and there being in the peace of God, and of the said Lord the King, and that he the said William Warren, with a certain hand gun of the value of twenty shillings, which he the said William Warren then and there held in both his hands, charges with gun powder and two leaden bullets, then and there, feloniously, willfully, and of his malice aforethought, did shoot off, and discharge at and against the said Crispus Attucks, and that the said William Warren, with the leaden bullets as aforesaid, out of the said gun powder, so shot off and discharges as aforesaid, did then and there, feloniously, willfully, and of his malice aforethough strike, penetrate, anwound the said Crispus Attucks in and upon his right breast,

The said Crispus Attucks then and there instantly died; and that the aforesaid Thomas Preston, William Wemms, James Hartegan, William M'Cauley, Hugh White, Matthew Killroy, William Warren, John Carrol, Hugh Montgomery, Hammond Green, Thomas Greenwood, Edward Menwaring, and John Munroe, then and there, feloniously, willfully, and of their malice aforethough, were present, siding, helping abetting, comforting, assisting, and maintaining the said William Warren, to do and commit the felony and murder aforesaid. x x x x

Then and there in manner and form aforesaid, feloniously, willfully, and of their malice aforethought, did kill and murder the said Crispus Attucks, against the peace of the said Lord the King, his crown and dignity.

JON. SEWALL, Att. pro. Dom. Rege. This is a true Bill. W. M. TAYLOR, Foreman x x x x

On Saturday, the 27th November, 1770, the Court being met, the prisoners were brought into Court and set to the bar, when the Court, proceeded thus.

Clerk of the Court read the indictment to them as before, to which they all pleaded not guilty.

Clerk. God send you a good deliverance!

The Jury were called over and appeared.

(Note: More than a hundred pages of testimony, in evidence, are omitted. The Editor).

x x x x

VERDICT

William Wemms, James Hartegan, William M'Cauley, Hugh White, William Warren, and John Carroll-- NOT GUILTY.

Mathew Killroy, and Hugh Montgomery, not guilty of murder, but GUILTY OF MANSLAUGHTER.

Wemms, Hartegan, M'Cauley, White, Warren and Carroll were immediately discharged: Killroy and Montgomery, prayed the Benefit of Clergy, which was allowed them, and thereupon they were each of them burnt in the hand, in open court, and discharged.

It may be proper here to observe, that Edward Manwaring, John Munroe, Hammond Green, and Thomas Greenwood, who were charged by the Grand Jury, with being present, aiding, abetting, assisting, etc. William Warren in the murder of Crispus Attucks, as is at large set forth in the Indictment, were tried on the 12th December following, and all acquitted by the Jury, without going from their seats.

(End of Trial Proceedings.)

25.[NO SLAVES WERE ADMITTED.]

[Hoping that the war would be short, the Negro slave, at first was excluded to prevent numerous enlistments for freedom through service. Also to draft slaves would have violated property rights of owners. Furthermore, to arm the slaves was considered a possible first step toward general freedom. Such were a few of the reasons authorities were slow to use Negroes in the Army.]

Proceedings of the Committee of Safety of Massachuette Bay.
Cambridge, 20th May, 1775.
In Committee of Safety--

Resolved-- That it is the opinion of the Committee, as the contest now between Great Britain and the Colonies respects the Liberties and Privileges of the Letter, and which the Colonies are determined to maintain, that the admission of any persons as soldiers into the army now raising, but only such as are Freemen,will be inconsistent with the Principles that are meant to be supported, and reflect Dishonor on this Colony, and that therefore no slaves be admitted into this Army upon any consideration whatever.' (Mass. MS Archives, Vol. 138, p. 67.)

26.[THE SLAVE WAS AGAIN DENIED ADMISSION TO THE ARMY]

Proceeding of the Provincial Congress of Massachusetts, June 6, 1775.

A resolve of the committee of Safety, relative to the (admission) of slaves into the Army was read, and ordered to lie on the table for further consideration.

(Journals of the Provincial Congress of Massachusetts, p. 302.)

27.[IN VARYING NUMBERS NEGROES FOUTHT FROM BUNKER HILL IN 1775 TO THE YORKTOWN SURRENDER IN 1783.]

Battle of Bunker Hill, June 17, 1775

"Nor should history forget to record that, as in the Army, at Cambridge, so also in this gallant band, the free Negroes of the colony (Massachusetts) had their representatives; for the right of free Negroes to bear arms in the public defense was at that day not disputed in New England. They took their place in the ranks with white men; and their names may be read on the pension rolls of the country,side by side with those of other soldier of the Revolution." (History of the United States, Bancroft, Vol. 4, p. 223.)

28.[GENERAL WASHINGTON INSTRUCTS RECRUITING OFFICERS NOT TO ACCEPT NEGROES, JULY 1775.]

Instructions for the Officers of the several Regiments of the Massachusetts Bay Forces, who are immediately to go upon the Recruiting Service.

You are not to enlist any deserter from the Ministerial Army, nor any stroller, Negro or vagabond, or person suspected of being an enemy to the liberty of America, nor any under eighteen years of age. As the cause is the best that can engage men of courage and principle to take up arms so it is expected that none but such will be accepted by the recruiting officers.

Given at Headquarters, at Cambridge, this 10th day of July, 1775.

Horatio Gates,
Adjutant General

(Force's American Archives, 4th Series, Vol. 2, p. 1630.) Washington took command of the Army at Cambridge on July 3, 1775 (Historical Notes by Rev. George H. Stone.)

29.[GENERAL WASHINGTON RECEIVES A LETTER.]

[Letter From J. M. Varnum to General Washington Suggests Raising One Battalion of Negro Soldiers]

Camp, January 2nd, 1778

Sir; The two battalions from the State of Rhode Island being small, and there being a necessity of the State's frunishing an additional number to make up their proportion in the Continental Army; the field officer have represented to me the propriety of making one temporary battalon from the two, so that one entire corps o entire corps oofficers may repair to Rhode Island, in order to receive and prepare the recruits for the field. It is imagined that a battalion of Negroes can be easily raised there. Should that measure be adopted, or recruits obtained upon any other principle, the service will be advance. The field officers who go upon this command, are Colonel Greene, Lieutenant Colonel Olney, and Major Ward. Seven captains, twelve lieutenants, six ensigns, one paymaster, one surgeon and mates, one adjutant and one chaplain.

I am, Your Excellency's most obedient servant,
J. M. Varnum

To His Excellency General Washington.
(Rhode Island Colonial Records, Vol. 8, p. 641.)

30.[GENERAL WASHINGTON RESPONDS TO A LETTER.]

[Letter From General Washington to Governor Cooke of Rhode Island suggests aid to General Varnum.]

Head Quarter, 2nd January, 1778.

Sir: Enclosed you will receive a copy of a letter from General Varnum to me, upon the means which this to be adopted for completing the Rhode Island Troops to their full proportion in the Continental army. I have nothing to say in addition to what I wrote the 29th of last month on this important subject, but to desire that you will give the officers employed in this business all the assistance in your power.

I am, with great respect Sir,
Your obedient servant,
G. Washington.

To Governor Cooke. (of Rhode Island) (R. I. Colonial Records, Vol. 3, p. 640.) letter of the 29th not found.

31.[THE BRITISH CONSIDER THE IDEA OF ARMING NEGROES AND INDIANS.]

Whitehall, August 2, 1775

My Lord; The hope you hold out to us in your letter of the first of May, that with a supply of arms and ammunition you should be able to collect from among the Indians, Negroes and other persons, a force sufficient, if not to subdue rebellion, at least to defend government, was very encouraging.

I am, my Lord, your Lordship's most obedient and humble servant,
Dartmouth,
(British Secretary of State for the American Department)
Earl of Dunmore.
(Royal Government of Virginia)

(Force's American Archives, 4th Series, Vol.3, p.6.)

32.[CAPTAIN COLLECT IS SUSPECTED OF ENCOURAGING SLAVE REVOLT, AUGUST 1775. MANY PERSONS LOYAL TO ENGLAND LOST LIVES, SLAVES, AND PROPERTY.]

Newbern (North Carolina) Committee,

In Committee, August 5, 1775.

x x x x

By a gentlemen just came to Town from Cape Fear, we have a certain account that the armed force which lately went down to burn Fort Johnson, have effected the same by destroying all the houses, and rendering theFort entirely useless. Captain Collect, who commanded the Fort, it is said, had a number of slaves, which he has instigated to revolt from their masters, actually concealed in the fort, which were again recovered by their several owners; for this treachery they burnt his dwelling house, with all his furniture, and everything valuable he had not time to get on board the man-of-war. (Force's American Archives 4th Series, Vol.111p.40)

33.[JOHN ADAMS WRITES ABOUT THE NEGROES.]

Extract from Diary of John Adams, Respecting an Interview with Mr. Bullock and Mr. Houston of Georgia, September 24, 1775.

These gentlemen give amelancholy account of the State of Georgia and South Carolina. They say that if one thousand regular troops should land in Georgia and their commander be provided with arms and clothesenough, and proclaim freedom to all the negroes who would join his camp, twenty thousand negroes would join it from the two Provinsec in a fortnight. The Negroes have a wonderful art of communicating intelligence among themselves; it will run several hundred miles in a week or fortnight. They say their only security is this: that all the King's friends, and tools of government, have large plantations, in property in Negroes; so that the slaves of the Tories would be lost, as well as those of the Whigs. (Works of John Adams, Volume 2, p. 428).

34.[A MOVE TO DISCHARGE ALL NEGROES IS LOST, SEPTEMBER 1775]

September 26, 1775. 'A debate occured in the Continental Congress upon the draft of a letter to thCommander-in-Chief reported by Lynch, Lee and Adams, to whom Several of Washington's previous letters had been referred, and E. Rutledge, of South Carolina, moved that the General should be instructed to discharge the Negroes, as well as slaves and freemen in his army. The resolution was lost! (Historial Notes, by Rev. Geo. H. Moore.)

The roll of army at Cambridge had, from its first formation, borne the names of men of color, but as yet without legislative approval.

On the Twenty-six September, 1775 Edward Rutledge, of South Carolina, moved to discharge all Negroes in the Army, and he was strongly supported by many of the southern delegates; but the opposition was so determined that he lost his point. (History of the United States, Bancroft, Vol. IV, p. 261.)

35. [THE COUNCIL OF WAR AGREES TO REJECT ALL NEGROES, OCTOBER 1775.]

At a Council of War, held at Headquarters (Cambridge, Mass.) October 8, 1775, present His Excellency General Washington; Major-General Ward, Lee and Putman; Brigadier Generals Thomas, Spencer, Heath, Sullivan, Greene and Gates, the question was proposed: 'Whether it will be advisable to enlist any Negroes in the new Army or whether there be a distinction between such as are slaves and by a great majority to reject Negroes altogether. (Notes on the employment of Negroes in the American Army of the Revolution, George H. Moore.))

36. [THE CONTINENTAL CONGRESS EXCLUDES THE NEGROES, OCTOBER 23, 1775.]

Proceeding of committee of conference at the camp at Cambridge, between General Washington and the representatives of Connecticut, Rhode Island, Massachusetts–Bay and the delegates of the Continental Congress.

October 23, 1775.

Ought not Negroes to be excluded from the new enlistment, especially such as are slaves? All were thought improper by the Council of Officers. Agreed, That they be rejected altogether." (Force's American Archives, 4th Series, Vol. III, p. 1161.)

37.[NEGROES HAVE PROVED THEMSELVES BRAVE.]

Extract from Letter of October 24, 1775 from General Thomas to John Adams.

"We have some Negroes, but I look on them, in general equally servicable with other men for fatigue; and, in action amny of them have proved themselves brave." (Hist. Negro Race in America. Williams Vol. I, p. 337).

38. [LORD DUNMORE ISSUES A PROCLAMATION, NOVEMBER 1775, AFTER GIVING UP HOPE FOR PEACE.]

By His Excellency the Right Honorable John, Earl of Dunmore, His Majest's Lieutenant and Governor General of the Colony and Dominion of Virginia, and vice Admiral of the same.

A PROCLAMATION.

And to the end that peace and good order may the sooner be restored, I do require every person capable of bearing arms to resort to His Majesty's standard, or be looked upon as traitors to His Majesty's Crown and Government, and thereby become liable to the penalty the law inflicts upon such offences - such as forfeiture of life, confiscations of lands, etc., etc., and I do hereby further declare all indented servants, Negroes or others, (appertaining to Rebels) free, that are able and willing to bear arms, they joining His Majesty's troops, as soon as may be, for the more speedily reducing this Colony to a proper sense of their duty to His Majesty's Crown and dignity.

Given under my hand on board the ship Williams, off Norfolk, the 7th day of November, in the sixteenth year of His Majesty's reign (1775).

Dunmore.

God save the King!

(Forces American Archives, 4th Series, Vol. III, p. 1385.)

39. [GENERAL WASHINGTON ORDERS THE EXCLUSION OF NEGROES, NOVEMBER 12, 1775]

Head Quarters, Cambridge, November 12th, 1775. Parole America. Countersign Freedom.

Neither Negroes, boys unable to bear arms, nor old men unfit to endure the fatigues of the campaign are to be enlisted.

(Washington's Orders, Vol. 1, p. 111, State Department.

40.[SOUTH CAROLINA AND ALL THE COLONIES USED THE NEGROES TO CONSTRUCT ROADS BATTERIES AND TO WORK AS ORDERLIES AND LABORERS IN MINES AND FIELDS.]

Proceedings of the Provincial Congress of South Carolina, November 20, 1775.

On Motion, resolved, that the Colonels of the several regiments of Militia throughout the Colony have leave to enroll such a number of able male slaves, to be employed as pioneers and laborers, as public exigencies may require, and that a daily pay of seven shillings and sixpence be allowed for the service of each such slave while actually employed.

(American Archives, 4th Series, Vol. 4, p. 62.)

41.[AFTER VERY LIMITED TRAININGG, SLAVES WERE TAKEN INTO BATTLE BY THE ENGLISH.]

Virginia, November 27, 1775.

Dear Sir:

The Governor (Dunmore, of Virgina) hearing of this, marched out with three hundred and fifty soldiers, Tories and slaves, to Kemp's Landing; and after setting up his standard, and issueing his proclamation, declaring all persons rebels who took up arms for the country, and inviting all slaves, servants and apprentices to come to him and receive arms, he proceeded to intercept Hutchings and his party, upon whom he came by surprise, but received, it seems, so warm a fire, that the ragamuffins gave way. They were, however, rallied on discovering that two companies of our Militai gave way, and left Hutchings and Dr. Reid with a volunteer company, who maintained their ground bravely till they were overcome by numbers, and took shelter in a swamp. The slaves were sent in pursuit of them; and one of Colonel Hutching's own, with another, found him. On their approach he discharged his pistol at his slave, but missed him; and was taken by them, after receiving a wound in his face with a sword. The numbers taken and killed, on either side, is not ascertained. It is said the Governor went to Dr. Reid's shop, and, after taking the medicines and dressings necessary for his wounded men, broke all the others to pieces. Letters mention that slaves flock to him in abundance, but I hope it is magnified.

I am, dear sir, Your most humble servant,

Edmund Pendleton,

To Richard Henry Lee.

(Force's American Archives, Fourth Series, Vol. IV, p. 202.)

42.[DEATH IS DECLARED FOR ANY SLAVES WHO ASSISTED THE ENGLISH, 1775.]

Proceedings of the General Convention of Virginia.
Tuesday, December 14, 1775.

Mr. Treasurer, from the Committee appointed to draw up a Declaration offering pardon to such slaves as should return to duty, reported that the committee had accordingly prepared the following Declaration; which he read in his place, and afterwards delivered in at the Clerk's table where the same was again twice read, and immediately agreed to:

By the Representatives of the people of the Colony and Dominion of Virginia, assembled in General Convention.

A DECLARATION

Whereas Lord Dunmore by his Proclamation, dated on board the Ship William, off Norfolk, the seventh day of November 1775, hath offered freedom to such able–bodied slaves as are willing to join him, and take up arms against the good people of this Colony, giving thereby encouragement to a general insurrection, which may induce a necessity of inflicting the severest punishment upon those unhappy people, already deluged by his ease and insidious arts; and whereas by an Act of the General Assembly now in force this Colony, it is enacted, that all Negro or other Slaves, conspiring to rebel or make insurrection, shall suffer death, and be excluded all benefit of clergy, we think it proper to declare that all slaves who have been or shall be seduced, by his Lordship's Proclamation, or other arts, to desert their master's service, and take up arms against the inhabitants of this Colony, shall be liable to such punishment as shall hereafter be directed by the General Convention. And to the end that all such sho have taken this unlawful and wicked step may retrun in safety to their duty, and escape the pùnishment due to their crimes, we heartily promise pardon to them, they surrendering themselves to Colonel William Woodford, or any other commander of our troops, and not appearing in arms after the publication hereof. And we do further earnestly recommend it to all humans and benevolent persons in this Colony to explain and make known this our offer of mercy to these unfortunate people. (Force's American Archives, Fourth Series, Vol. 4, pp. 84, 85.)

43.[GENERAL WASHINGTON STATES THAT LORD DUNMORE SHOULD BE CRUSHED FOR PROMISING FREEDOM TO NEGROES.]

Camp, December 15, (1775).

Dear Sir:

If the Virginia's are wise, that arch–traitor to the rights of humanity, Lord Dunmore, should be instantly crushed, if it takes the force of the whole Colony to do it–other–wise, like a snow–ball, in rolling, his army will get size, some through fear, some through promises, and some through inclination, joining his standard; but that which renders the measure indispensably necessary, it is the Negroes–for if he gets formidable, numbers of them will be tempted to join who will be afraid to do it without.

I am, dear sir, Your affectionate humble servant,
George Washington,

To Joseph Reed.
(Life and Correspondence of Joseph Reed, Vol. 1, p. 136).

44. [THE NEGROES MADE 'FIRST CLASS SOLDIERS.']

The Subscribers begs leave to report to Your Honorable House (which we do in justice to the character of so brave a Man) that under Our Own observation, We declare that A Negro Man, Called Salem Poor of Col. Frye's Regiment, Captain ames Company, in the late Battle at Charlestown, behaved like an Experienced officer, as Well as an excellent Soldier, to Set forth Particulars of his Conduct would be Tedious. We would only beg leave to say in the Person of this said Negro centors a Brave and gallant soldier, the reward due to so great and Distinguished a Character, we submit to the Congress.

Cambridge, December 1st, 1775.
"To the Honorable General Court of "Massachusetts Bay."

45.[FREE NEGORES ARE PERMITTED TO ENLIST, AFTER A PROTEST.]

Cambridge, December 31, 1775.

Sir: x x x x x x x x x x
It has been represented to me that free Negroes who have served in this Army are very much dissatisfied at being discarded. As it is to be apprehended that they may seek employ in the Ministerial Army, I have presumed to depart from the resolution respecting them, and have given license for their being enlisted. If this is disapproved by Congress, I will put a stop to it. -x -x- -x- -x- -x- -x- -x-

I have the honor to be your most obedient
and humble servant,
George Washington,

To the Honorable John Hancock, Esq.'
(President of Congress)
(Force's American Archives, 4th Series,
Vol. 4, p. 485.)

46.[GENERAL WASHINGTON REVERSES HIS ORDER AND ALLOWS FREE NEGROES TO ENLIST PENDING APPROVAL BY CONGRESS.]

HeadQuarters, Cambridge, Dec. 30, 1775.

Parole Marblehead. Countersign Manty.

x x x x x x x

As the General is informed that numbers of free Negroes are desirous of enlisting, he gives leave to the recruiting officers to entertain them, and promises to lay the matter before Congress, who he doubts not will approve it. -x- -x- -x- -x- -x- -x- -x-

(Washington's Orders, Vol. 1, p. 149, State Department.)

47. [FREE NEGROES WHO HAVE SERVED MAY REENLIST.]

January 16, 1776 - Proceedings of the Continental Congress

"The Committee on General Washington's letters brought in a report, which being taken into consideration, the Congress thereupon came to the following resolution: -x- -x- -x- -x- -x-

That the free Negroes who have served faithfully in the Army at Cambridge may be reinlisted therein but no other." (Journals of Congress, Vol. 2, pp 23-26). The Comm. was composed of Mr. Wythe, Mr. Adams, and Mr. Wilson."

48. [A MINISTER SUGGESTS FREEING THE SLAVES TO WIN THEIR SUPPORT DURING THE WAR.]

"Rev. Dr. Hopkins, of Rhode Island, wrote: God is so ordering it in his providence, that it seems absolutely necessary something should speedily be done with respect to the slaves among us, in order to our safety, and to prevent their turning against us in our present struggle, in order to get their liberty. Our oppressors have planned to gain the blacks, and induce them to take up arms against us, by promising them liberty on this condition; and this plan they are prosecuting to the utmost of their power, by which means they have persuaded numbers to join them. And should we attempt to restrain them by force and severity, keeping a strict guard over them, and punishing them severely who shall be detected in attempting to join our opposers, this will only be making bad worse, and serve to render our inconsistence, oppression and cruelty more criminal, perspicuous, and shocking, and bring down, the righteous vengence of heaven on our heads. The only way pointed out to prevent this threatening evil is to set the blacks at liberty ourselves by some public acts and laws and then give them proper

I am your Excellency's most humble servant.
N. Green.

encouragement to labor, or take arms in the defense of the American cause as they shall choose. This would at once, be doing them some degree of justice, and defeating our enemies in the scheme that they are prosecuting.

49.[TWO CAPTURED NEGROES WERE FREED FROM SLAVERY; HOWEVER, THE SYSTEM OF SLAVERY WAS NOT CONDEMNED NOR CHANGED.]

It so happened that shortly afterward (1776) two Negro men, taken prisoners at sea, were advertised to be sold at public auction at Salem. Indignation and sympathy were aroused. A resolution was offered in the Massachusetts, House of Representatives to the affect that 'the selling and enslaving of the human species is a direct violation of the natural rights, alike vested in all men by their Creator and Utterly inconsistent with the avowed principles on which this and the other United States have carried their struggle for liberty even in the last appeal, and that therefore all persons connected with the said Negroes be, and they are hereby forbidden to sell them, etc. It is to be remarked that the resolution eventually passed omitted the foregoing general declaration of anti-slavery principle, and simply forbade the sale of the two men. (The Civil War in America, John W. Draper, Vol. 1, p. 316)

50.[A LETTER FROM N. GREEN TO GENERAL WASHINGTON.]

Camp on Long Island,
July 21, 1776, two o' clock.

Sir:

A Negro belonging to one Strickler, at Gravesend, was taken prisoner (as he says) last Sunday at Coney Island. Yesterday he made his escape, and was taken prisoner by the rifleguard. He reports eight hundred Negroes collected on Staten Island, this day to be formed into a regiment.

To his excellency, General Washington
Headquarter's, New York.

(Forces American Archives, Fifth Series, Vol. I, p. 486)

51. [FEVER AND DEATH AMONG NEGROES EXCEEDS THAT OF THE ENGLISH.]

Ship Dunmore, In Gwin's Island, Harbor, Va.
June 26, 1776. x x x x x

I am extremely sorry to inform your Lordship that fever, of which I informed you in my letter No. 1, has proved a very maligant one, and has carried off an incredible number of our people, especially the blacks. Had it not been for this horrid disorder, I am satisfied I should have had two thousand blacks with whom I should have had no doubt of penetrating into the hearts of this colony.

Dunmore.

To Lord George Germaine. (Force's American Archives, 5th Series, Vol. 2, 162.)

52.[DURING THE FIRST YEAR OF THE WAR' NEW HAMPSHIRE EXCLUDED NEGROES FROM MILITARY SERVICE.]

Act of the Legislature of New Hampshire.

– – – – – –

An Act for forming and regulating the Militia within the State of New Hampshire, in New England, and for repealing all the laws heretofore made for that purpose.

x x x x

And be it further Enacted by the Authority aforesaid, that that part of the Militia of this State commonly called the Training Band, shall be constituted of all able bodied Male Persons there in, from sixteen years old to fifty, excepting Negroes, Mulattoes, and Indians.

x x x x

Passed September 19, 1776.
(Acts and Laws of New Hampshire, 1776 to 1780. pp. 36 & 43.)

53. [THE QUAKERS AND NEGROES ARE EXEMPTED, NOVEMBER 1776]

Act of the Legislature of Massachusetts.

'An Act for the providing a Reinforcement to the American Army.'

x x x x x x

'And it is enacted by the Council and House of Representatives in General Court assembled and by the Authority of the same.

That no Rank or Station in Life, Place, Employment or Office (except as hereinafter accepted, shall excuse or exempt any Person from serving in Arms for the Defense of his Country, either by himself or some ablebodied effective Man in his stead, or in case of his Neglect or Refusal , from paying the fine hereinafter required.

Provided nevertheless, that those persons who had before the nineteenth day of April, 1775, been by Law deemed to be of the Denomination of Christians called Quakers, settled Ministers of the Gospel, the President, Professors, Tutors, Librarian, and Under Graduates of Harvard College, Indians, Negroes and Mulattoes, shall not be held to take up Arms or procure any person to do it in their Room.' Passed November 14th, signed November 15th, 1776. (Laws of Massachusetts July, 1775, to October 1789, p. 89.)

54. [SOUTH CAROLINA'S VAST NEGRO LABOR RESERVE WAS EXTENSIVELY REGULATED. THE NEGRO POPULATION, AT TIMES, WAS TWO TO ONE COLONISTS.]

February 14, 1777. The General Assembly of South Carolina passed an ordinance entitled 'Ordinance to carry into effect an 'Ordinance to direct the manner of procuring Negroes to be employed in the public service, 'passed October 9, 1776. This Ordinance was designed to further regulate the manner of procurement of slaves for labor on the public works. (Statutes at Large, S. C., pub. in 1838, Vol. 4, p. 394.)

55. [NEGRO VOLUNTEERS TO THE ENGLISH EXCEED THE WHITES. FREEDOM WAS EXPECTED BY THE NEGROES. IN ACTUAL PRACTICE, THE ENGLISH DID NOT ALWAYS FREE THE SLAVES.]

Lord Dunmore to the Secretary of State.
Ship 'Dunmore' in Elizabeth River, Va.
30th March, 1776.

Your Lordship will observe by my letter, No. 34, that I have been endeavoring to raise two regiments here,-- one of white people, the other of black. The former goes on very slowly, but the latter very well, and would have been in great forwardness, had not a fever crept in upon them, which carried off a great many very fine fellows.

(Force's American Archives, Fifth Series, Vol. 2, p. 160.)

56. [FREE NEGROES ARE RECRUITED AS DRUMMERS OR AS PIONEERS. A PIONEER IS A FORWARD COMBAT MAN.]

Act of the General Assembly of Virginia.
An Act for regulating and discipling the Militia.

– – – – – – – –

For Forming the citizens of this Commonwealth into a militia and discipling the same for defense thereof, Be it enacted by the General Assembly, That all free male persons, hired servants, and apprentices between the ages of sixteen and fifty years (except xxxxshall by the commanding officer of the county in which they reside, be enrolled or forced into companies of not less than thirty-two, nor more than sixty-eight, rank and file. x x x x The free Mulattoes in the said companies or battallions shall be employed as drummers, fifers or pioneers x x x x x

Passed at a Session begun and held May 5, 1777.
(Henning's Statutes of Virginia, Vol. 9, pp. 267-268.)

*Here follow exemption, among which Negroes or persons of color do not appear.

57. [FREEDOM THROUGH MILITARY SERVICE WAS NOT APPROVED.]

"In May, 1777, the General Assembly of Connecticut appointed a Committee to take into consideration the state and condition of the Negro and mulatto slaves in this State, and what may be done for their emancipation. This Committee, in a report at the same session (signed by the Chairman, the Honorable Matthew Griswold, of Lyme, recommended–

"That the effective Negro and mulatto slaves be allowed to enlist with the Continental Battalions now raising in this State, under the following regulations and restrictions: viz., that all such Negro and mulatoo slaves as can procure, either by bounty, hire, or in any other way, such a sum to be paid to their masters as such Negro or mulatto shall be judged to be reasonally worth by the elect men of the town where such Negro or mulatto belongs, shall be allowed to enlist into either of said Battalions, and shall therefore be de facto free and emancipated; and that the master of such Negro or mulatto shall be exempted from the support of maintenance of such Negro or mulatto in case such Negro or mulatto shall hereafter become unable to support and maintain himself.

"And that in case any such Negro or Mulatto slave shall be disposed to enlist into either of said Battalions during the war, he shall be allowed so to do: and such Negro or mulatto shall be appraised by the select men of the town to which he belongs; and his master shall be allowed to receive the bounty to which such slaves may be enlisted, and also one-half of the annual wages of such slave during the time he shall continue in said service;providedhowever, that said matter shall not be allowed to receive such part of said wages after he shall have received so much as amounts, together with the bounty, to the sum at which he was appraised.

"This report in the Lower House, was ordered to be continued to the next session of the Assembly. In the Upper House it was rejected.

"Mr. Trumbull writes; You will see by the Report of Committee, May 1777, that General Varnum's plan for the enlistment of slaves has been anticipated in Connecticut; with this difference, that Rhode Island adopted it, while Connecticut did not.

"The two States reached nearly the same results by different methods.

x x x x x x x

"In point of fact, some hundreds of black slaves and freemen were enlisted from time to time, in the regiments of the State troops and of the Connecticut line. How many, it is impossible to tell; for from first to last, the company or regimental rolls indicate no distinction of Color. The name is the only guide; and, in turning over the rolls of the Connecticut line, the frequent recurrence of names which were exclusively appropriate to Negroes and slaves, shows how considerable was their proportion of the Continental Army; while such surnames as Liberty, Freemen, Freedom, &c., by scores, indicate with what anticipation, and under what inducements, they entered the service."

(J. Hammond Trumbull, Editor of the Public Records of the Colony of Connecticut as quoted by Livermore in An Historical Research pp. 113 to 116.)

58. [FOUR NEGROES RELEASED FROM ARMY FOR RETURN TO SLAVERY, 1777. SUCH A WAVERING POLICY EXISTED UNTIL JANUARY, 1863.]

Head Quarters Boston June 25, 1777.

Gentlemen.

Captain Stephen Ketchum of the Island of Bermuda, has just made complaint to me that some Time the last winter or Spring one Captain Hardy of Woburn in this State in a privteer took a Sloop belonging to said Island, out of which he took the Cargo, and four Negro's called slaves who were hands on Board and whom he the said Harding brought to this place, and afterwards Enlisted, or rather sold into a Company raising by Captain Danforth of Bilerica, receiving for them the Continental, States & Towns Bounty. Captain Ketchum having lately arrived at this port with a load of Salt from Bermuda, hearing of the affair and knowing one of the Negro's and the manner in which the matter had been conducted, request the release of the Negro's, whom he desires to return to their Masters. I think it my duty to discharge them from the Army, and as Captain Hardy has received the different Bounties, I think it my duty also to acquaint your Honors of the proceeding that such steps may be taken as to you in your Wisdom may seem meet to secure said Bounties.

I am very respectfull
Your Honors
Obedient Servant.
W. Heath

Council June 26, 1777
Read & Sent down
J. O. Avery Dpy Secy
Council of Mass'tts Bay
(Manuscript Archives of Mass., Volume 197, p. 197.)

59. [SEGREGATION IS RECOMMENDED FOR NEGRO SOLDIERS, AUGUST 27, 1777]

Extract from letter of Brigadier-General W. Heath to Honorable Samuel Adams, dated at Boston, August 27, 1777, relative to troops that had marched from Massachusetts to reinforce the Army at Ticonderoga.

"As to the Ability of Body of the men I cannot fully determine the greater part that I saw appeared able- But it is more than probable that there were some men advanced in life and some Lads, and a number of Negroes, the latter were generally ablebodied but for my own part I must confess I am never pleased to see them mixed with white men."

(Mass. MS. Archives, Volume 215, p. 236.)

60. [NEGROES WERE USED IN ABUNDANCE]

[This extract shows how extensive the use of the Negro was, although records don't always indicate the race of the soldiers]

"Extract from the Journal of a Hessian Officer, October 23, 1777, Relating to the Use of Negroes in the American Army.

The Negro can take the field instead of his master; and therfore no regiment is to be seen in which there are not Negores in abundance; and among them there are able-bodied, strong and brave fellows." (An Historical Research, Livermore, P. 111).

61. [LETTER OF THOMAS KENCH RECOMMEND NEGROES BE ALLOWED TO FIGHT FOR FREEDOM AGAINST THE ENEMY, 1778]

The letter I wrote before I heard of the Disturbence with Col. Sears, Mr. Spear, and a number of other Gentlemen Concerning the freedom of Negroes In Congress Street. It is a pitty that Riots should Be committed on the Occation, as it is justifiable that Negroes Should have their freedom and None amongst us be held as Slaves as freedom and Liberty is the great Controversy that we are Contending for and I trust under the smiles of Divine province we shall obtain it if all our minds Can But Be united and putting the Negroes Into the Service will prevent much uneasiness and give more Satisfaction to those that are offended at the thoughts of their Servant Being free, I will not Inlarge for fear I should give offense. But Subscribe my Self your faithful Servant

Thomas Kench Castle Island April 7, 1778

(Manuscript Archives of Mass. Volume, 199, p. 84.)

62. [NEGROES ARE NOT ALLOWED TO REENLIST IN RHODE ISLAND]

Proceedings of the General Assembly of the State of Rhode Island and Providence Plantations, May Session, 1778.

Whereas, by an Act of this Assembly, Negro, Mulatto and Indian Slaves, belonging to the Inhabitants of this state, are permitted to enlist into the Continental Battalions, ordered to be raised by this state; and are thereupon forever manumitted and discharged from the service of their Master; and whereas, it is necessary, for answering the purpose intented by the said act, that the same should be temporary.

It is therefore voted and resolved, that no Negro, Mulatto and Indian slave, be permitted to enlist into said Battalions, from and after the 10th day of June, next and that the said act then expire, and be no longer in force; anything there is to the contrary notwithstanding.

(Rhode Island Colonial Records, Volume 8, p. 399.)

63. [SEVEN HUNDRED NEGROES FOUGHT ALONG WITH THE WHITES AT THE BATTLE OFMAMMOUTH, N.J. JUNE 28, 1778]

Battle of Mammouth, N. J.
June 28, 1778.

Nor may history omit to record that of the revolutionary patriots who on that day periled life for their country, more than seven hundred colored Americans fought side by side with the white. *(Bancrof's History of the United States Vol. 5, p. 277.) *See Army Returns of August 24, 1778.

64. [A SUGGESTION TO RAISE 3000 NEGROES IS NOT APPROVED.]

Letter of J. Rutledge, Governor of South Carolina, to the delegates of the State. April 24, 1779. Received May 17.

Charles Town, April 24, 1779.

Gentlemen:

As soon as I received the Resolve of Congress respecting the raising 3000 Negroes, I called a full Council and communicated it to them.

The proposition was unanimously rejected. One Governor Homan was for raising 1,000, but his motion was disagreed to by the other eight members of the Council.

The Assembly stands adjourned to the 10th May–I doubt whether they will meet then, but, if they whould I am rather inclined to think they will not, at present, adopt such a measure.

I am Cen.t your Very most obedient servant.

J. Rutledge

The Delegates of South Carolina in Congress.
(State Papers. Vol. 72, p. 491, State Department.)

65. [THE BRITISH PROCLAMATION PROMISES SECURITY TO NEGROES WHO COME OVER TO THEIR SIDE]

By His Excellency Sir Henry Clinton, K. B. General and Commander–in–Chief of all his Majesty's Forces within the Colony laying on the Atlantic Ocean, from Nova Scotia to West Florida, inclusive, etc., etc., etc.

'Proclamation'

Whereas, the enemy have adopted a practice of enrolling Negroes among their Troops, I do hereby give notice, That all Negroes taken in arms, or upon any military duty, shall be purchased for (the public service) at a stated Price; the money to be paid to the Captors.

But I do most strictly forbid any Person to sell or claim Right over any Negro, the property of a Rebel, who may take refuge with any part of this Army; and I do promise to every Negro who shall desert the Rebel Standard, full security to follow within these lines, Any occupation which he shall think proper.

Given under my hand, at Head Quarters, Phillipsburgh, the 30th day of June, 1779, by His Excellency's command.

H. Clinton,
John Smith, Secretary.

66. [A LETTER OF JAMES MADISON TO JOSEPH JONES]

James Madison To Joseph Jones
Philadelphia, November 23, 1780.

Dear Sir:

Yours of the 18th came yesterday. I am glad to find the Legislature persist in their resolution to recruit their line of the army for the War; though without deciding on the expediency of the mode under their consideration, would it not be as well to liberate and make soldiers at once of the blacks themselves, as to make them instruments for enlisting white soldiers? It would certainly be more consonant to the principles of liberty, which ought never to be lost sight of in a contest for liberty; and with white officers and a majority of white soldiers, no imaginable danger could be feared from themselves, as there certainly would be none from the effect of the example on those who should remain in bondage; experience having shown that a freedman immediately loses all attachment and sympathy with his former fellow–slaves. (Madison Papers, Vol. 1. p. 68.)

67. [ACT OF THE GENERAL ASSEMBLY OF NEW JERSEY EXEMPTS SLAVES FROM MILITARY SERVICE, 1781]

Act of the General Assembly of New Jersey. An act for the regulating, training and arraying of the Militia, and for providing more effectually for the Defense and Security of the State. Passed June 8, 1781.

x x x x x x x

1a. And be it further Enacted; That the Captain or Commanding Officer of each Company shall keep a true and perfect List or Roll of all effective Men between the Aged of sixteen and Fifty years, residing within the District of such Company. Provided always, That x x x x slaves and every Person exempted by any particular Law of this State, shall not be borne on any such Lists or Rolls, or be subject to Military duty. x x x x x x x

Laws of New Jersey by Peter Wilson, Trenton, 1784. pp. 166-168-169.

68. [THE BRITISH ORDERED TWO REGIMENTS OF NEGROES RECRUITED IN SOUTH CAROLINA.]

Headquarters, High Rock Ford, on Haw River 28 February, 1781.

Sir:

x x x x x x x

The enemy have ordered two regiments of Negroes to be immediately embodied, and are drafting a great proportion of the young men of that State (South Carolina), to serve during the war.

x x x x x x x

I have the honor to be, with esteem and respect, &c.

Nathaniel Greene,

(To General Washington.)
(Sparks' Correspondence of the American Revolution, Vol. 3 p. 244.)

69. [NEGRO SOLDIERS DEFEND THEIR COMMANDER TO THE DEATH, 1781.]

"When Colonel Greene was surprised and murdered, near Points Bridge, New York, on the 14th of May, 1781, his colored soldiers heroically defended him till they were cut to pieces, and the enemy reached him over the dead bodies of his faithful Negroes."

(An Historical Research, Livermore, p. 207.)

70. [A LETTER OF JOHN CADWALDER TO GENERAL GEORGE WASHINTON REPORTS HIS ACTION TO RAISE NEGRO TROOPS.]

Annapolis, 5 June, 1781.

Dear Sir:

We have resolved to raise immediately, seven hundred and fifty

Negroes, to be incorporated with the other troops; and a bill is now almost completed.

x x x x x x x

With the greatest esteem, nc.,
John Cadwalder

(To General Washington)
(Sparks' Correspondence of the American Revolution,
Vol. 3, p. 329).

71. [RESOLUTIONS ARE SUBMITTED]

"Report of the Committee on the Motion of the Delegates of Georgia, Delivered December 8, 1780, Read. August 24, 1781 - Not to be Acted Upon."

"The Committee to whom was referred the Motion from the delegates of Georgia - beg leave to report - That the several acts of the 29th March 1779, recommending the Levy of Blacks for the defense of Georgia and South Carolina, were never received by the Legislature of the former and consequently could not be carried into execution by that State. That although the measure was not adopted in South Carolina at that time - The necessity of the present juncture, and the difficulty of completing the Continental Quotas of those States in the ordinary method makes it incumbent on them to employ this resource for their own and the General Interest.

"Your Committee therefore submit the following Resolutions - viz: Resolved - That an officer be appointed to Levy a Corps of one thousand able-bodied Negroes in Georgia and South Carolina under the authority of the Executives of those States, and that the said Executives be required to give every possible support to the measure.

"Resolved - That the said Corps be officered and organized under the direction of the Commanding Officer of the Southern Department, who is to give every necessary assistance in procuring the said Levies.

"That the officers be taken from such as may be spared from the Continental Line in the first instance, and then from reduced officers.

"The preference being given to those of Georgia and South Carolina in proportion to the number of Levies obtained, which officers are to be entitled to the same pay and emoluments as other officers of equal rank in the Continental Army.

"Resolved - That the conditions offered to the Black Soldiers be the same as expressed in the Act of the 29th of March, 1779, and that Congress will make provision for paying a reasonable price to the proprietors of such Negroes, provided they be not adherents to the enemy.

"Resolved - That the Board of War be directed as soon as possible to procure and send forward a sufficient number of Arms and accoutrements, together with the necessary clothing, for the said Corps."

(Reports of Committee on State Papers, Vol. 2, p. 443, No. 20, State Department.)

72. [SUGGEST KING OF ENGLAND AUTHORIZE TEN THOUSAND BLACKS, 1782. THE ENGLISH WERE IN GREAT NEED OF MENN.]

EARL OF DUNMORE TO SIR HENRY CLINTON, 1782.
Charles Town, Feb. 2, 1782

'Sir:

I was in hopes of having the pleasure of delivering the enclosed letters in person, but the fleet in which I came out not proceeding to New York, being advised, and thinking it unsafe to hazard a further voyage to the northward, at this season of the year, with so large a fleet.

x x x x

'I arrived here the 21st of December; and having no employment, I made it my business to converse with every one that I thought capable of giving me any good information of the real situation of this country; and every one that I have conversed with think, and I must own, my own sentiments perfectly coincide with theirs, that the most efficacious, expeditious, cheapest and certain means of reducing this country to a proper sense of their duty is in employing the blacks, who are, in my opinion, not only better fitted for service in this warm climate than white men, but they are also better guides, may be got on much easier terms, and are perfectly attached to our sovereign. And, by employing them, you cannot devise a means more effectual to distress your foes, not only by depriving them of their property, but by depriving them of their labor. You in reality deprive them of their existence; for, without their labor, they cannot subsist; and, from my own knowledge of them, I am sure they are as soon disciplined as any set of raw men that I know of.

x x x x

"What I would further propose is, that the officers of the Provincials, who are swarming in the streets here, perfectly idle, should be employed to command these men, with the rank they now have.

"I would also propose, at first, to raise only ten thousand Blacks, to give them white officers and non-commissioned officers, but to fill up the vacancies of the non-commissioned officers now and then with black people, as their services should entitle them to it.

'In order to induce the Negroes to enlist, I would propose to give each black man one guinea and a crown, with a promise of freedom to all that should serve during the continuance of the war; and, that they may be fullysatisfied that this promise will be held inviolate, it must be given by the officer appointed to command them, he being empower so to do, in the most ample manner, by your Excellency.

x x x x x x x

'Should this plan in general meet with your Excellency's approbation, there are many more ideas relative to it that I will take another opportunity of communicating to you.

'I have wrote fully to Lord George Germain on this subject, and have sent him a copy of this letter, but I hope, before we can hear from home, you will have had the credit of adopting the plan.'

73.[THE ENGLISH SUGGEST USING THE NEGRO AS A SOLDIER]

Earl of Dunmore to Secretary Lord George, Germain.
Charles Town, S.C., March 30, 1782

Since writing to your Lordship of the 5th of February, there has been a motion made in the Rebel Assembly of this Province for raising a brigade of Negores, which was only negetived by a very few voices, and it's supposed will be resumed and carried on a future day; and we, by neglecting to make a proper use of those people, who are much attached to us, shall have them in a short time employed against us. They are now carring them up the country as fast as they can find them.

(An Historical Research, Livermore, p.147.)

74.[WASHINGTON'S LETTER TO COLONEL JOHN LAURENS SPEAKS OF SELFISH INTEREST OF PEOPLE AFTER THE WAR]

Washington to Col. John Laurens.
Head Quarters, 10th July, 1782.

My dear Sir:

The last post brought me your letter of the 19th of May. I must confess that I am not at all surprised at the failure of your plan. The spirit of freedom, which, at the commencement of this contest, would have gladly sacrificed everything to the attainment of its object, has long since subsided, and everselfish passion has taken its place. It is not the public, but private, interests which influence the generality of mankind; nor can the Americans any longer boast an Exception. Under these circumstances, it would either have been surprising if you had succeeded; nor will you, I fear, have better success in Georgia. (Sparks' Washington, Volume 8, pp. 322-323.)

INFANTRY AND DRUMMER
1775 to 1815

THE BLACK MINUTEMAN
1775

CHAPTER 4

THE BLACK SOLDIER DURING THE POST REVOLUTIONARY WAR PERIOD

The Revolutionary War was won by the United States; and the policy of utilizing Negroes in the military fluctuated. After the Revolutionary War, in 1792, Congress restricted service in the National Militia to "free able bodied white male citizens." Generally, the states conformed to this policy. The Negroes were not called to service, in considerable numbers, until the English landed again on U.S. soil during the War of 1812 to 1815. After this war was won, Negroes were again excluded from military service until the civil war in 1861-1865.

Military contributions of Negroes during both wars; the publicity about freedom and equality; and influence of the abolitionists in state legislatures shortened the era of slavery in Northern states. In 1780, Pennsylvania and Massachusetts abolished slavery; in 1783, New Hampshire abolished slavery; and in 1784, Rhode Island and Connecticut abolished slavery. The federal congress was still dominated by pro-slavery men until the 1850's and 1860's.

75. [AFTER THE WAR ENDED, SOME SLAVES WHO FOUGHT WERE FREED.]

In New Hampshire those blacks who enlisted for three years were manumitted. (Notes on Employment of Negroes in the American Army of the Revolution, Moore.) No date was shown. Manumitted, means to be freed. (Editor)

76. [AN ACT TO FREE SLAVES WHO WERE PROMISED FREEDOM FOR MILITARY SERVICE BUT WHO HAD BEEN REENSLAVED, AFTER THE WAR, BY FORMER OWNERS.]

Act of Virginia Legislature at Session begun October 20, 1783: 'An Act directing the emancipation of certain slaves who have served as soldiers in this State, and for the emancipation of slave Aberdeen.'

'Section I. Whereas it hath been represented to the present General Assembly, that during the course of the war, many persons in this State had caused their slaves to enlist in certain regiments or corps raised within the same, having endered such slaves to the officer appointed to recruit forces within the State, as substitutes for free persons, whose lot or duty it was to serve in such regiments or corps, at the same time representing to such recruiting officers that the slaves so enlisted by their direction and concurrence, were freemen; and it appearing further to this Assembly, that on the expiration of the term of enlistment of such slaves, that the former owners have attempted again to force them to return to a state of servitude, contrary to the principles of justice, and to their own solemn promise. And whereas it appears just and reasonable that all persons enlisted as aforesaid who have faithfully served agreeable to the terms of their enlistment, and have thereby of course contributed towards the establishment of American liberty and independence, should enjoy the blessing of freedom as a reward for their toils and labors;

'Section 2. Be it therefore enacted, That each and every slave, who by the appointment and direction of his owner, hath enlisted in any regiment or corps raised within this State, either on Continental or State establishment, and hath been received as a substitute for any free person whose duty or lot it was to serve in such regiment or corps, and hath served faithfully during the term of such enlistment, or hath been discharged from such service by some officer duly authorized to grant such discharge, shall from and after the passing of this Act, be fully and completely emancipated,and shall be held and deemed free in as full and ample a manner as if each and every of them were specially named in this Act; and the Attorney General for the Commonwealth, is hereby required to commence in action, in Forma Paupers, in behalf of any of the persons above described who shall after the passing of this Act be detained in servitude by any person whatsoever; and if upon such prosecution it shall appear that the pauper is entitled to his freedom in consequence of this Act, a jury shall be empannelled to assess the damages for his detention. And whereas it has been represented to this General Assembly, that Aberdeen, a Negro man slave, hath laboured a number of years in the public service at the lead mines, and for his meritorous services is entitled to freedom.

'Section 3. Be it therefore enacted, That the said slave Aberdeen shall be and he is hereby emanicipated and declared free in as full and ample a manner as if he had been born free.' (Jefferson's collection laws of Va., Vol. 6, Session October, 1783, pp. 6-7.)

77. [NEGROES NEVER RECEIVED BOUNTY PROMISED AFTER WAR]

Rhode Island Battlion: "They seem never to have received the bounty which the law under which they enlisted promised to them; a pretext being set up that their liberty was biven to them in lieu of bounty. Nor do they appear ever to have received the allowance given the white soldier for the depreciation of the money in which they were paid, Finally it appears that they were deprived of large sums due them as wages by means of forged orders." (An Historical Inquiry concerning the attempt to raise a regiment of Slaves by Rhode Island during the War of the Revolution, by Sidney S. Rider. Prefatory Remarks)

78. [AFTER THE REVOLUTIONARY WAR, NEGROES WERE REJECTED, AS SOLDIERS.]

Act of the General Court of Connecticut.

An Act for the forming, regulating and conducting the Military Force of this Stae.

Whereas the defense and Security of all Free States depends (under God) upon the Exertions of a well regulated and disciplined Militia; Wherefore Be it Enacted by the Governor, Council and Representatives, in General Court assembled and by the Authorities of the Same. That all Male Persons, from Sixteen Years of Age to Forty-five, shall constitute the Military Force of this State, except x x x x and, Indians, Negroes and Mulattoes.

Revision of 1784, date of original Enactment not discovered.

(Elisha Babcock, print, p. 144.)

79. [FREE NEGROES WERE REQUIRED TO SERVE IN STATE MILITIA AFTER THE WAR, 1784]

Act of the General Assembly of Virginia.

An Act for amending the several laws for regulating and disciplining the militia and guarding against invasions and insurrections.

x x x x x x x x

I. Be it enacted that all free persons between the ages of eighteen and fifty years, (except x x x x x x x) shall be enrolled or formed into companies. x x x x x x Passed at the session begun and held October 18, 1784. (Hennings Statutes of Virginia, Vol. II. pp. 476-477.)

II. Here follow a list of exemption, in which Negroes, or persons of color, are not included.

80. [CARE FOR POOR AND DISABLED NEGROES IS AUTHORIZED IN RHODE ISLAND, 1785.]

Act of Rhode Island Legislature.

An Act for the support of the Paupers, who heretofore were slaves and enlisted into the continental Battalions.

Whereas, during the late war it was thought expedient, by the Legislature, to raise a Corps to serve in the Continental Battalions, by enlisting the slaves within this State: And whereas, since disbanding the said Corps, many of the said soldiers have become sick, and otherwise were unable to maintain themselves; and as they have gained, no legal Place of Settlement, it is necessary that provision should be made for their support, and that no particular Town should be overburthened with them:

Therefore, Be it enacted by this General Assembly, and by the Authority thereof it is enacted, that when and so often as it shall happen, that any Indian, Negro or Mulatto, who was heretofore a slave, and enlisted into and served in the Continental Battalions in the pay of this State, by virtue of an Act of this Assembly passed at the Session in February, A. D. 1778, shall become sick, or otherwise unable to support and maintain himself, it shall be the duty of the Town-Council of the Town where such Indian, Negro, or Mulatto, who was heretofore a slave, and enlisted into the Continental Battalions as aforesaid, and shall be sick or otherwise unable to support and maintain himself, to direct the Overseers of the Poor of such Town to Take Care of and Provide for such sick or poor Indian, Negro, or Mulatto, in the same Way, and with the same Economy and Frugality, as though such Indian, Negro or Mulatto, was a Pauper of the said Town. And the Town Council of the Town where such Indian, Negro or Mulatto, shall be sick, or otherwise become poor, and unable to maintain himself shall adjust the Accounts of such Overseers of the Poor, for the Maintenance and Support of such sick or Poor Indian, Negro or Mulatto, who was heretofore a slave, and lay the same before the General Assembly: And if such Accounts are reasonable, just and right, they shall be paid out of the General Treasury.

And be it further enacted, That whenever and so often as it shall happen, that such Indian, Negro or Mulatto, shall be supported in any other way than is hereinbefore prescribed, it shall be at the proper Cost and Charge of the person or Persons who shall keep and provide for him of them. (Rhode Island Acts, Session Feb. 1785, p. 16.)

81. [NEGROES ARE REJECTED AFTER REVOLUTIONARY WAR, IN 1785, IN MASSACHUSETTS.]

Act of the General Court of Massachusetts: An act for regulating and governing the Militia of the Commonwealth of Massachusetts, and for repealing all laws heretofore made for that purpose.

I. -x- -x- -x- -x- That the several laws heretofore made for regulating the militia aforesaid, be, and hereby repealed.

II. -x- -x- -x- -x- That the said Militia shall be formed into a train–band and alarm–list; to contain all trained and ablebodied men, from sixteen to forty years of age, and the alarm–list, all other men under sixty years of age, excepting in both cases such as shall be hereafter by this Act exempted.

XLIII. -x- -x- -x- -x- Negroes, Indians, and Mulattoes, shall be, and hereby are exempted from both the train-band and alarm-list aforesaid. Passed March 10, 1785. (Perpetual Laws of Massachusetts from October 1780 to May, 1789, pp. 338, 339, 348.)

82. [ALL FREEMEN AND INDENTURED SERVANTS MUST SERVE. 1786.]

Act of the General Assembly of North Carolina.

An Act for establishing a Militia in this state.

Whereas, in all republican Governments a well regulated Militia is highly necessary for the defense and safety thereof:

I. Be it enacted therefore by the General Assembly of the State of North Carolina, and it is hereby enacted by the authority of the same, That all Freemen and indented servants within this State, from eighteen to fifty years of age, shall compose the militia thereof. -x- -x- -x- -x- -x- (Passed at Session Begun November 18, 1786. Iredell's Revisions of the Laws of North Carolina, 1791. p. 591.)'

83.[NEGROES WERE RECRUITED WITHOUT ARMS, IN 1788 AS DRUMMERS, TRUMPETERS AND PIONEERS.]

Act of the General Assembly of Virginia.

An Act for the better regulation of the Militia.

II. Be it therefore enacted, by the Lieutenant Governor, Council, and Burgesses, of this present General Assembly and it is hereby enacted by this authority of the same, that from and after this publication of this act, the colonel or chief officer of the militia in every county shall list all free male persons above the age of one and twenty years within this colony under the command of such captain.

V. And be it further enacted by the authority aforesaid, that every person, so as aforesaid listed, (except free Mulattos, Negroes, and Indians) and placed or ranked in horse or foot, shall be armed and accoutred in manner following:

VI. And be it further enacted, that all such free Mulattos, Negroes, or Indians, as are or shall be listed, as aforesaid shall appear without arms; and may be employed as drummers, trumpreters, or pioneers, or in such other senile labour, as they shall be directed to perform.

Passed at session begun August 1, 1788. (Hennings Statue of Virginia, Vol. 5, pp. 16-17.)

84. [AFTER THE WAR ENDED, THE NATIONAL LAW EXCLUDED NEGROES; RESTRICTED SERVICE TO ABLE-BODIED WHITE MEN.]

Act of the Congress of the United States of May 8, 1792.

An act more effectually to provide for the National Defense by establishing a uniform Militia throughout the United States.

Section I.. Be it enacted by the Senate and House of Representatiges of the United States of America in Congress assembled.

That each and every free able-bodied white male citizen of the respective States, resident therein, who is or shall be of the age of eighteen years, and under the age of forty-five years, (except as hereinafter excepted,) shall, severally and respectively, be enrolled in the Militia -x- -x- -x- -x- -x- -x- -x- -x-

Approved May 8, 1792. (U.S. State. at Large, Vol. 1, p. 271).

Note the Militia Laws of the States were generally made to conform to the act of Congress: but see the laws of North Carolina, South Carolina, and Georgia and Louisiana.

– – – – – – – –.

85. [NEGROES ARE RECRUITED AS FATIGUEMEN AND AS PIONEERS 1794.]

Act of the General Assembly of South Carolina.

An Act to organize the Militia throughout the State of South Carolina, in conformity with the Act of Congress.

Whereas, it is necessary to organize the Militia of this State in conformity with the Act of Congress in that case made and provided.

x x x x x x x x

33. And be it further enacted by the authority aforesaid, That all free Negroes and Indians, (nations of Indians in amity with the State excepted,) Moors, Mulattoes and Mestizoes, between the ages of eighteen and forty-five, shall be obliged to serve in the said Militia as fatigue men and pioneers, in the several regimental beats in which they reside; and upon neglect or refusal to attend when summoned on duty, they, and every one of them, shall be liable to the like penalities and forfeitures as privates in the same regimental company are made liable by law.

x x x x x x x x

Passed May 10, 1794.
(McCord's Statutes of South Carolina, Vol. 8, pp. 485, 496.)

CHAPTER 5

THE BLACK SOLDIER DURING THE WAR OF 1812

Although England and the United States signed the Treaty of 1783, England was slow to recognize the independence of the United States and indicated her unwillingness in many ways. England continued to hold military posts on the western frontier, and was suspected of passing arms to incite the Indians against the U. S. During the Napoleonic War, England's Naval recruiting system, men were impressed forcefully into the English Navy; they were flogged in discipline. To escape severe punishment, many British Sailors deserted, and entered the United States merchant marines because the pay was better. The British declared that a British subject had no rights to enter the military nor merchant marine service of any country, and that they could take an Englishman from ships or from land wherever they found him. Accordingly, they ordered their ship Captains to stop American ships at sea. Both countries were English speaking, so Americans were sometimes kidnapped from vessels. English ship captains also kidnapped Negroes, Swedes, Danes, and Portuguese from American ships. The English bombarded some American Ships. This kidnapping, and other acts, led to friction and to the War of 1812.

By 1812 the economy minded Presidential Administration after Washington had reduced the size of the U. S. Army to less than 3,000 men. Few were Negroes. Both men and officers were poorly disciplined and were not selected from the most reliable element of the population; consequently, the English secured temporary victories at Detroit, Baltimore, Washington, D. C., New Orleans, and on other costal towns. But the U. S. Navy, under younger and more vigorous leadership, did well against the British at sea. Nearly 20% of the U. S. Navy personnel was Negros.

During the land encounters, Negro regulars, volunteers, and reserves were called into service in New York, Baltimore, Washington, D. C., Philidelphia, and in New Orleans. Negroes volunteered in large numbers hoping to share in the aim of freedom. They fought until the War ended; however, in 1820, recruiting officers were instructed not to enlist Negroes. Until the mid-Civil War era in 1863, few Negros were enrolled in the Army, and were held in slavery.

One Postwar advantage of the War of 1812 was that it cultivated a stronger feeling of national untiy among the people of the United States. The western, northern, southern and people of the original eastern colonies fought together in unity. Only the Negro was excluded; the Negro who, in 1860, was to become the focal point of division of this new unity in a dreadful Civil War.

Documents of the military services, of 200,000 Negro soldiers during the Civil War are more numerous than during previous periods and is the material for several other books to be written by the editor.

86. [LOUISIANA ACTS TO ORGANIZE FREE MEN 1812]

Act of the Legislative of Louisiana.

An Act to organize a Corps of Militia, for the service of the State of Louisiana, as well for its defense as for its police, a certain portion of chosen men from among the free men of colors.

Be it enacted by the Senate and House of Representatives of the State of Louisiana in General Assembly covened, That the Governor of the State of Louisiana is authorized by virtue of the present Act, to organize in a Corps of Militia, as soon as he may judge proper, for the defense of this State, certain free men of color, to be chosen from among the Creoles, and from among such as shall have paid a State tax. The Commander-in-Chief shall provide for the choice of their officers; Provided, however, that their Commanding officer shall be a white man; and for the manner of arming them, and he shall prescribe the kind of Discipline which to him may appear most conductive to the success and good order of the said Corps, Provided, always, that the said Corps shall not consist of more than four companies, each of which, officers included, shall not consist of more than sixty-four men, and that such as shall enter into said corps must have been for two years previous thereto, owners, or sons of owners, of landed property of at least the value of 300 dollars." Approved September 6, 1812.

(Acts of the General Assembly of La., passed at its first Session, 1814, p. 72).

87. [A LETTER FROM WILLIAM LEE TO THE WAR DEPARTMENT SEPTEMBER, 1814. HE ESTIMATES THE COST OF MAINTAINING A NEGRO SOLDIER WOULD BE HALF AS MUCH AS A WHITE MAN]

Georgia, Jasper County, 5 'sept., 1814.

Dear Sir:

The lamentable news of the destruction of our Capitol has this moment reached us. Whilst I join the thousands of our country in bewailing the humiliating and heart-burning catastrophe, I shall not think my feelings lowered by offering my sincere congratulations on the danger you have escaped.

In the prosecution of a savage war such as the enemy is now waging against us, all the means of defense which are not injurious to our probity or courage allowable.

On our Magnanimity and humanity the enemy has no claim except for his women and children, and even this he ought not to expect.

My motive for Liberty I am taking, is to offer a suggestion for the benefit of our country which I fear your Excellency will think a little wild if not dangerous.

This is the employment of Negroes in the present war.

We already believe that the enemy is training Negroes for the purpose of arming them against us, and we already know that he has armed the ruthless savage, not only against our warriors, but against our women and children.

If the practice can be justified by honour, the following considerations will fix the economy and safety.

The bounty and pay fo a soldier for five years is not less than $900. His clothing must be regularly furnished, his pay regularly made up, his rations good and in full quantity, or he becomes mutinous.

A Negro man can be purchased for a little more than half of this sum. If he is half as well fed and half as well clad as a white man, he will be satisfied. With regard to our safety; the employment of such force so far from endangering of us, will be greater means of lessening our danger in the Southern States. Let an offer of liberty be made to those who are willing to serve during the war, and I think it will not fail to call from amongst us all those from whom, we apprehend an insurrection. Let this force be sent against Canada and it would enable us to increase our defense on the sea coast.

The greatest difficulty which offers in the present case is the disposition of those slaves at the termination of the war. Might they not colonize some part of Louisiana and be made a territorial part of our government?

Though I scarely dare to think of it, yet I dare to ask; is it not probable that the termination of new feuds may put it in our power to offer them a settlement still farther from home? There are numbers of freed Negroes in the Northern States, who if they were permitted would probably strengthen our lines and when the soldiery was to be colonized, would furnish them with wives and citizens. Many of the more industrious of those who survived the war would in a series of years be able to purchase their progeny from their former masters, by which the interests of humanity would be greatly promoted. If in addition to this, there was a country to which freed slaves might be sent, it would be a great inducement to the benevolent to free them.

At a moment like this, when the feelings of your Excellency and of every American are burning with indignation, these suggestions may claim your consideration. With full assurance that they will meet all the respect which they deserve, I subscribe myself,

Your Excellency's very humble Servant
Will. Lee.

Letters Rec'd, War Dept. Sept., 1814.

88. [A LETTER FROM A CITIZEN SUGGESTED RECRUTING A REGIMENT OF NEGRO SOLDIERS, 1814.]

New York,
6th September, 1814

Sir:

Some two or three inhabitants of this town apprehending a probability that some additional troops will be voted at the ensuring session of Congress have expressed a novel idea. x x x x x x x x

It was supposed that as there is a very considerable black (or colored) population in this place who have a stake in society it might be feasible to raise an effective regiment of that description that officers of ability, intelligence, and standing among the whites would readily be found that the non-commissioned officers should be colored men that such a corps would meet a reduced bounty with alacrity.

Such is the outline of the plan-if it should Meet the approbation of the War Department,I would wish to be considered an applicant for a company. x x x x x x x x

Sir,
Yr. Mo. Obdt. Servt.
Thos. Lefferts

(Letters Received. War Department, September 1814.)

89. [GENERAL ANDREW JACKSON RECRUITS NEGROES FOR THE EMERGENCY ONLY.]

Proclamation

To the free colored inhabitants of Louisiana.

Through a mistaken policy you have herefore been deprived of a participation in the glorious struggle for national rights in which our country is engaged. This no longer shall exist.

As sons of freedom you are called upon to defend our most inestimiable blessing. As Americans your country looks with confidence to her adopted children for a valorous support, as a faithful return for the advantages enjoyed under her mild and equiable government. As farthers, husbands and brothers, you are summonded to rally rounnd the Standard of the Eagle, to defend all which is dear in existance.

Your country, although calling for your excertions, does not wish you to engage in her cause without amply renumerating you for the services rendered. Your intelligent minds are not to be led away by false representations. Your love of honor would cause you to despise the man who should attempt to decieve you. In the sincerity of a soldier, and the language of truth, I address you.

To every noble hearted, generous freeman of color, voluteering to serve during the present contest with Great Britain, and no longer, there will be paid the same bounty in money and lands now received by the white soldiers of the United States, viz: $124 in money, and 160 acres of land. The non-commissioned officers and privates will also be entitled to the same monthly pay and daily rations and clothes furnished to any American soldier.

On enrolling yourselves in companies, the Major-general commanding will select officers for your government, from your white fellow citizens. Your non-commissioned officers will be appointed from among yourselves.

Due regard will be paid to the feelings of freemen and soldiers. You will not, by being associated with white men, in the same corps, be exposed to improper comparisons or unjust sarcasm. As a distinct independent battalion of regiment, pursuring the path of glory, you will undivided, receive the applause and gratitude of your countrymen.

To assure you of the sincerity of my intentions and my anxiety to engage your invaluable services to our country, I have communicated my wishes to the Government of Louisiana, who is fully informed as to the manner of enrollment, and will give you every necessary information on the subject of this address.

Headquarters, 7th Military District,
Mobile, Sept. 21st, 1814
Andrew Jackson
Maj. Gen. Commanding

Niles Weekly Register, Dec. 3, 1814

90. [NEW YORK LEGISLATURE ACT TO RAISE MEN OF COLOR]

Act of the Legislature, New York.

Act to authorize the raising of two regiments of men of Color of which the following are extracts:

'I. Be it enacted by the people of the State of New York, represented in Senate and Assembly, That the Governor of the State of New York be, and he is hereby authorized to raise, by voluntary enlistment, two regiments of free men of color, for the defense of the State, for three years, unless sooner discharged.

'II. And be it further enacted, That each of the said regiments shall consist of one thousand and eighty able-bodied men; and the said regiments shall be formed into a brigade, or be organized in such a manner, and shall be employed in such service, as the Governor of the State of New York shall deem best adapted to defend the said State. x x x x x x x x

'VI. And be it further enacted, That it shall be lawful for any able-bodied slave, with the written assent of his Master or Mistress, to enlist into the said corps, and the master or mistress of such slave shall be entitled to the pay and bounty allowed him for his service; and further, that the said slave, at the time of receiving his discharge, shall be deemed and adjudged to have been legally manumitted from that time, and his said master or mistress shall not thenceforward be liable for his maintenance. x x x x x x x x

Passed October 24, 1814.
(Laws of New York, Chapter 18. 38th Section.)

Note - That Adjutant General of New York, in a letter to the War Department, state that the records of his office do not show that any enlistments were made under this Act of the State Legislature.

91. [GENERAL JACKSON MAKES A REPORT. NEGRO TROOPS FROM ST. DOMINGO WERE BRAVE]

Extract from report of Major General Andrew Jackson relative to the action of a portion of his forces at Villere's Plantation, below New Orleans on the night of the 23rd of December, 1814.

Headquarters 7th Military District,
Camp below New Orleans,
27th December, 1814, in the morning.

Sir: x x x x x x x x

I was resolved to attack his (the enemy's) first position, with Major Hinds' dragoons-General Coffee's brigade - part of the 7th and 44th Regiments - the uniformed company of militia under the command of Major Planche - 200 men of color, chiefly from St. Domingo, raised by Colonel Lavery and acting under the command of Major Dagwin (D'Aquine) and a detachment of Artillery under the direction of Colonel McRae, with two six pounders under the immediate command of Lieutenant Spots - not exceeding in all 1500. x x x General Coffee was ordered to turn their right, while with the remainder of the forces, I attacked his strongest position on the left near the river. x x x In this affair the whole corps under my command deserve the greatest credit. x x x Lavery's Volunteers manifested great bravery. x x x x x x x

I have the honor to be with great respect,

Your obedient servant,
Andrew Jackson,
Major-General, Commanding.

To: Hon. James Monroe
Secretary of War.

92. [GENERAL JACKSON PRAISES EVERY CORPS UNDER HIS COMMAND]

Headquarters, 7th Military District,
Camp 4 miles below New Orleans,
2nd January, 1815, 8 o'clock, AM

Sir:

On yesterday the enemy opened upon us a tremendous cannonade from several batteries which they had erected on the night preceeding. It was sustained by every corps under my command with a firmness which would have done honor to veterans. x x x x x x x x

I have the honor to be, very respectfully,

Your obedient servant,
Andrew Jackson,
Major General, Commanding.

Honorable James Monroe
Secretary of War.

93. [GENERAL JACKSON PRAISES THE FIRMNESS OF HIS TROOPS.]

Extract From Report of Major General Andrew Jackson about the Battle of New Orleans, 1815 x x x x x x x x

Camp 4 miles below Orleans,
9th January, 1815.

Sir: x x x x

In my encampment every thing was ready for action when early on the morning of the 8th, the enemy, after throwing a heavy shower of bombs and congreve rockets, advanced their columns on my right and left to storm my entrenchments. I can not speak sufficiently in praise of the firmness and deliberation with which my whole line received their approach. More could not have been expected veterans innured to war.

I have the honor to be, with great respect,
Your obedient servant,
Andrew Jackson,
Major-General, Commanding.

94. [THE ADJUTANT GENERAL ROBERT BUTLER PRAISES NEGRO TROOPS SERVICE.]

General Orders
Headquarters 7th military District,
Camp below New Orleans,

Adjutant General's Office, January 21, 1815.

Before the camp at these memorable times shall be broken up, the General thinks it a duty to the brave army which has defended them, publicly to notice the conduct of the different corps which compose it. x x x x x x x x

The two corps of colored volunteers have not disappointed the hopes that were formed of their courage and perseverance in the performance of their duty. Major Lacoste and Daquin, who commanded them, have deserved well of their country. Captain Savary's conduct has been noticed in the account rendered of the battle of the 23rd, and that officer has since continued to merit the highest praise. x x x x x x x x

By Command
Robert Butler
Adjutant General

Niles Weekly Register
February 25, 1815

CHAPTER 6

THE U. S. POPULATION
1619-1815
and the
AFRO-AMERICAN

Between 1607 and 1815, the United States expanded from a population of 120 Englishmen at Jamestown, Virginia to a population of more than three million in 1815; from one small town to 13 colonies extending from New Hampshire to Georgia, and from the Atlantic Ocean to the Rocky Mountains in the West. During this period slavery existed to a degree in the 13 colonies. The Negro population expanded from 20 to more than 500,000 during the same period.

Along with population and territorial expansion, military conflicts were almost continuous for the first 200 years. In addition to local military encounters between the expanding colonies and the Indians, the United States participated in 70 years of active warfare - nine historical wars. The manpower drain was very heavy; every able-bodied man was needed on the home and on the military front.

For the first 200 years misfortune was a companion of the earliest British North American colonists as they struggled to cultivate their new surroundings. In May 1607, Christopher Newport landed in Virginia and laid our Jamestown. He brought 120 men, searching for gold and for trade. During the first year, the 120 men were reduced to 40 by diseases, hunger, poor management, internal conflict, and by Indian attacks. Part of the suffering was due to the lack of laborers. Most of the original colonists were gentlemen and were not accustomed to hard work. Generally, Indians did not submit to slavery. Population growth was slow. By 1619, less than 2,000 colonists of 10,000 new arrivals, survived misfortunes in Virginia. In 1619, ninety "young maidens" were sent over from England to Jamestown; the first representative government in the colonies was organized; and the Negro was introduced into the colony at Jamestown, Virginia. Farming and commerce began to improve. The Negro proved to be vital; he was introduced into the colonies in increasing numbers.

Working on outlying plantations, on road building, and in forest clearing, Negroes were exposed to military attacks, sometimes before the colonists of the inner forts. Due to this exposed position, the Negro had to fight for local defense or to try to escape slavery, or to be captured. Many farmers, ranchers, and colonists slept soundly because of the protection provided partly by Negroes in a military capacity, either as militiamen or as civilians, Later, national unity, continental, and overseas expansion was made easier partially through the help of Negro servicemen.

In the meantime, other territorial areas of the United States were being settled by the English. Religious and political persecution in Europe gave impetus to population growth in the Colonies. In 1620, the pilgrims landed in Plymouth, Mass; in 1630, the Puritans landed in Salem, Mass., in 1634, the Calvanist landed in Baltimore, Maryland. By 1650 Virginians ventured southward into North Carolina; in 1664, the Dutch settled in New York, and in 1681, the Quakers settled in Pennsylvania. Between 1628 and 1640, 20,000 people came to the New Colonies. In the 13 colonies a few people were royal representatives, some were trademen, some were indentured servants; and some were slaves. In 1770, Virginia had a population of 450,000, 50% of whom were slaves; Maryland had a population of 200,000, 1/3 of whom were slaves; South Carolina had two slaves to one colonist. In 1754,.the total British populatin 1,500,000, the French population in Canada and the Mississippi Valley was only 100,000. By 1775, the population of the 13 colonies was more than 3 million of which 501,000 were Negro slaves; 50,000 Negroes were in the north. Territorial expansion, diseases, hunger, constant military conflict in the colonies and in Europe required an increasing number of able-bodied men. The Negro contributed primarily to commercial and geographical expansion and to a minor extent to military defense in all the colonies and later to the United States.

Negro slavery was introduced during the era of conflict, and was abolished in the original thirteen colonies as indicated below:

NOTE: From the Negro Yearbook - 1912.

Date Introduced	Date Abolished	Colony
1619	1865	Virginia
1626	1827	New York
1628	1846	New Jersey
1630	1780	Massachusetts
1631	1784	Connecticut
1636	1865	Delaware
1647	1784	Rhode Island
1634	1865	Maryland
1665	1865	South Carolina

1669	1865	North Carolina
1670	1783	New Hampshire
1681	1780	Pennsylvania
1750	1865	Georgia

95.[THE SLAVE POPULATION INCREASE WITH THE NEED FOR LABOR.]

SLAVE POPULATION, 1715

In 1715 the royal governors of the colonies gave the Board of Trade the number of the Negroes in their respective colonies. The slave population was as follows:

New Hampshire	150	Pa. and Delaware	2,500
Massachusetts,	2,000.	Maryland,	9,500
Rhode Island,	.500.	Virginia,	.23,000
Connecticut,	1,500.	North Carolina,	3,700
New Jersey,	1,500.	South Carolina,	15,000.
New York,	4,000.		
		Total	.58,850

(History of the Negro Race in America, Williams, Vol.1, part 3.)

96.[AS SHOWN BELOW THE NEGRO POPULATION BY 1775 HAD INCREASED CONSIDERABLY.]

SLAVE POPULATION

When the Revolution had begun, the slave population of the thirteen colonies was as follows:

Massachusetts	3,500
Rhode Island,	.4,373.
Connecticut,	.5,000.
New Hampshire,	629.
New York,	.15,000.
New Jersey,	.7,600.
Pennsylvania,	.10,000.
Delaware,	.9,000.
Maryland,	.80,000.
Virginia,	.165,000.
North Carolina.	.79,000.

South Carolina, ...110,000.
Georgiaa, ...16,000.

(History Negro Race in America, Williams, Vol.1, p.355.)

97. [THESE RETURNS DID NOT SHOW ALL NEGROES WHO SERVED.]

RETURN OF NEGROES IN THE ARMY. AUGUST, 1778

Brigades	Present	Sick Absent	On Com.	Total
North Carolina	42	10	6	58
Woodford	36	3	1	40
Muhlenburg	64	26	8	98
Smallwood	20	3	1	24
2nd Maryland	43	15	2	60
Wayne	2	-	-	2
2nd Pennsylvania	33	1	1	35
Clinton	33	2	4	39
Parsons	117	12	19	148
Huntington	56	2	4	62
Nixon	26	-	1	27
Patterson	64	13	12	89
Late Learned	34	4	8	46
Poor	16	7	4	27
	586	98	71	755

Alex Seammell,
Adj. Gen'l.

(History Negro Race in America, Williams, Vol. 1, p. 36.) This Return evidently included only the colored enlisted men in the army under the immediate orders of the Commander–in–chief. It did not include the Rhode Island Battalion. (Note: Race was not shown on many records. The Editor)

98. [BATTLE CASUALITIES ARE REPORTED]

Negroes are Listed Among Battle Casualties, 1639.

'7th, 25th, 1639. A list of the men that slain in a fite at Fallmoth & all soe how many was wounded in said fight. x x x x x x x x x

An Indian.

An Negro of Colo Tyngs.'

(Massachusetts MS Archives, Vol. 36, p. 15.)

These men do not appear on the list of slain and it is to be inferred that they were among the wounded.

(This is one of the earliest casulty reports
in U. S. history.)

99. [PRIMUS AMONG THE EARLIEST BATTLE CASUALTIES.]

An Account of the Dead, Dismist, killed and taken belonging to his Majesties Service from December ye 25th, 1724, to April ye 24th, 1725.

'Dead -x- -x- -x- Primus, Negro---------Capt. Moodey. -x- -x- -x- -x- -x- -x-

(Mass. MS Archives. Vol. 72, p. 226.)

100.[THIS IS AMONG THE FIRST WOUNDED REPORTS ON NEGRO SOLDIERS DURING THE REVOLUTIONARY WAR.]

Battle of Lexington

The following is a list of those provincials who were killed, wounded and missing in the action of the nineteenth of April, 1775, and the towns to which they respectively belong; including all that were lost that day. -x- -x- -xx- -x- -x- -x-

Lexington-----Wounded;x x x Prince, Negro.
(Journals of the Provincial Congress of
Mass, 1774-5, pp. 678-9.

INFANTRY AND BANDSMAN
1775-1815